Samuel Ireland

Picturesque Views on the River Wye,

from its source at Plinlimmon Hill, to its junction with the Severn below Chepstow:

with observations on the public buildings, and other works of art, in its vicinity

Samuel Ireland

Picturesque Views on the River Wye,
from its source at Plinlimmon Hill, to its junction with the Severn below Chepstow: with observations on the public buildings, and other works of art, in its vicinity

ISBN/EAN: 9783337233679

Printed in Europe, USA, Canada, Australia, Japan

Cover: Foto ©Thomas Meinert / pixelio.de

More available books at **www.hansebooks.com**

PICTURESQUE VIEWS

ON THE

RIVER WYE.

Course of the RIVER WYE from its Source to its junction with the SEVERN below Chepstow.

Picturesque Views
ON THE
RIVER WYE,
FROM
Its Source at Plinlimmon Hill, to its Junction
WITH THE
SEVERN below CHEPSTOW:
WITH
OBSERVATIONS
ON
THE PUBLIC BUILDINGS, AND OTHER WORKS OF
ART, IN ITS VICINITY:

BY SAMUEL IRELAND,
AUTHOR OF
" A Picturesque Tour through Holland, Brabant, and part of France;"
AND,
Of " Picturesque Views on the Rivers Thames, Medway,
" Warwickshire Avon," &c.

London:
PUBLISHED BY R. FAULDER, NEW BOND STREET;
AND T. EGERTON, WHITEHALL.

1797.

PREFACE.

AMONGST the numerous rivers with which our Island is so richly ornamented and fertilized, the Wye, our present subject of investigation, though in no very widely extended course, and itself only a tributary stream, is yet in the production of the sublime, of the grand and majestic proudly eminent above its fellows. In a course of about eighty miles, the utmost distance it measures from its source, to its junction with the Severn, so various and such an interesting picturesque scenery is perhaps no where

where to be found, either in this or any other country.

Nature and Art have most happily combined in opening their richest stores to diversify and spread fertility, grandeur and beauty over the country through which it flows: for its environ is not less highly distinguished and dressed by the hand of art with castles, abbies, and villas beautifully seated on its banks, than it is itself favoured by nature, in the striking interchange of shoal and flood, wood and rock, meadow and precipice. With so much, and in so many various ways to allure and interest, it was not possible that all its charms could have escaped either the penetrating eye of Taste and Genius, or the pencil of the inquisitive, refined, and systematical Amateur,

and

and accordingly many of its most striking features have employed the pens and the pencils of our Writers and Artists; but they have, all of them, been either detached views and single objects, or, if more has been comprehended in the design of the amateur or artist, the execution has been partial, imperfect, or foreign to the subject. The whole has never been fully exhibited to the eye of the lover of the scenes of nature faithfully delineated. One ingenious author indeed has given observations upon the river, and such as have unquestionably merited the high commendations they have received from the admirers of the picturesque and beautiful: and he has accompanied his observations with drawings. He does not however profess to give exact representations, or portraits of the various objects that present themselves, but aims rather at exhibiting their general effect on the eye, when confidered technically, and as picturefque forms by the learned and profeffed artift.

WITHOUT interfering therefore with the plan of that much admired writer, or arrogating to himfelf fuperior fcience or knowledge of his fubject, the author of this work has, in conformity with his original intention, felected this river from amongft thofe not yet defcribed, in order to complete his hiftory of the principal rivers of this country: and, unable as he feels himfelf to render juftice to the dignity of his fubject, he builds his claim to public favor, on the fidelity with which he flatters himfelf he has delineated the fcenery. He would

would wish, and it is his aim, that his drawings should, like the transparent mirror of his stream, truly reflect the landscape that exists around, as well as the objects that decorate its banks. And, content with the simple charms and varieties of nature, he cannot prevail upon himself to contemplate in every winding of the stream the forms of his own idea, the image of his own mind and its complicated sameness, reflected again, and again; but gives to his reader that, which, if he visits the spot, he trusts he will find, and, if the spot is known to him already, he assures himself he will recognize.

The tremendous floods, which, in the beginning of the year 1795, subsequent to that, in which these drawings were made,
having

having so completely swept away several ancient, as well as elegant structures thrown across this stream, may perhaps give some additional value to the sketches of them here introduced. If not elsewhere preserved, scarce a vestige of them remains to be resorted to by the artist or by the architect, whose profession must peculiarly enable him to do more justice to the nature of the fabric.

The History, and Picturesque Views of the River Severn are in great forwardness, and will, it is presumed, be ready for publication, in Two Volumes, Royal Octavo, in the course of next year.

PRINTS

Picturesque Views

ON THE

RIVER WYE.

"Plinlimmon's high praife no longer Mufe defer;
"What once the Druids told, how great thofe floods fhould bee,
"That here (moft mightie hill) derive themfelves from thee.
"The Bards with furie rapt, the Britifh youth among,
"Unto the charming harpe, thy future honor fong
"In brave and loftie ftraines :———"

DRAYTON.

SECTION I.

FROM a small spring near the summit of Plinlimmon Hill, the boundary of the northern part of Cardiganshire, our river Wye derives its source. Issuing from a spacious hollow in this mountain, the water falls in a narrow streamlet several hundred yards nearly

nearly perpendicular, till meeting with various small currents, it soon presents itself in the shape of an immense cataract, rolling with astonishing rapidity over the rocky prominencies which seem to impede its course. The name of this river appears anciently to have been a common appellation, either for river or water. Camden says, that the word gwy or wy signifies water, and instances the following names which have that termination, as proofs of his opinion; viz. Lhugwy, Dowrdwy, Edwy, Conwy, Elwy, Towy, Tawy, &c. &c. From the same ridge of mountains, within two miles of the source of the Wye, the rivers Severn and Rydall derive their origin: the latter of which empties itself into the Irish sea at Aberystwith. The views from this huge and dreary hill are wild and extensive beyond description; they exhibit mountains, rolling as it were, over each other, and under the most sublime forms and
beau-

beautiful hues, varying and shifting till they insensibly lose themselves and melt into the horizon. We were peculiarly fortunate in having a bright and clear day to view in all its grandeur this sublime and picturesque scenery; an advantage which an experienced guide informed us had scarce ever occured during a course of many years in those airy regions, where it was almost invariably his fate to encounter a heavy and hazy atmosphere, commonly attended with rain. On this lofty mountain the famous Owen Glyndwr, in the summer of 1401, posted himself, says the historian, " with great policy " at the head of a hundred and twenty men " of arms." The situation of Plinlimmon Hill being on the limits of Cardiganshire and Montgomeryshire, was admirably adapted for receiving the succours of his vassals and friends from every part of the principality. From this fastness his adherents, who were the terror of all that opposed him, were perpetually

petually making excursions, and plundering the neighbouring counties; amongst which Montgomeryshire appears to have been the greatest sufferer.

The birth of this renowned hero, of Wales, which happened on the 28th of May, 1354, appears by Hollingshed and others, to have been marked with strange presages of celebrity: he says, that his cruelty was foretold at his nativity, by the wonderful circumstance of " his father's " horses being found standing that night in " the stable up to their bellies in blood;" and Shakspeare, in the following lines, put into the mouth of Glyndwr, thus describes the vain glorious chieftain,

> ─────── " At my birth
> " The front of Heav'n was full of fiery shapes;
> " The goats ran from the mountains, and the herds
> " Were strangely clamorous in the frighted fields:
> " These signs have marked me extraordinary,
> " And all the courses of my life do shew,
> " I am not in the roll of common men."

A still

A still more extraordinary circumstance is attached to the history of this Welch phænomenon. Jolo Goch, a celebrated bard, has not hesitated to consider the great event of his birth, as equal in importance to mankind with that of Jesus Christ.

The river Wye, in this its earliest stage, is peculiarly marked with features of the grand and sublime: its amazing rapidity is perpetually interrupted by immense large stones and rocky substances, and the rush of its waters produces a solemn noise, that seems as if they were

"Chiding the stones that stopp'd their course."

The spots of verdure and broken ground in the vicinity of this rude scene, the dark shades of rock, and beetling brows of the hills with which it is bounded on either side, form a spectacle as majestic and awful as the

the untaught imagination can paint, or that can prefent itfelf to the eye throughout the range of this ifland.

It is fimple nature in her pureft and grandeft form, and without a trace of her handmaid art, without either caftle, church, or ruin: objects that more than form the beautiful in picture, that are effentially neceffary, and can alone give dignity to the feeble works of man: without thefe the fcenery is here complete.

For feveral miles the country wears nearly the fame afpect; one continued undulating line of hills forms the diftance; and the river, though of no confiderable width, continues gently to roll over its rocky and gravelly bed, " making fweet " mufic with the enamelled ftones;"

"Giving a gentle kifs to every fedge
"He overtaketh in his pilgrimage."

At a distance of about six miles from its source, in a village called Cumergar, the Wye receives a considerable body of water from the river Castal. This River is full in view, and forms a beautiful object from the road, on the way to what is called the Devil's Bridge. At Cumergar is a wooden bridge called Pont-rhyd Gallad: it is the first that is thrown across this river, and the scenery around it is extensive and beautiful. The Wye here loses much of its impetuosity and consequently of its grandeur: its rocky bed is softened and in many places spread with a mere gravelly substance, and at this summer season is considerably narrowed, and frequently left perfectly dry. From the continual accession, however, of springs and rills, that issue from the neighbouring mountains, it is not known to remain long in that state. From hence, on an easy ascent, a tolerable road leading to Llanidlos runs parallel with the stream, and affords a beautiful ride

side till we approach the wretched village of Llangerig: amongst whose clay cottages without chimneys, churlish boors, and four milk and black bread, the only refreshment it supplied, our weary spirits were filled with rapture at the beauties of that situation, to which extreme penury, savage nature, or insensibility could alone be indifferent: They were so impressive, that within a mile of this village we determined to stop, flattering ourselves with the hope that by the aid of the pencil, we might be enabled to give the characteristic features of a country, which we utterly despair by any powers of language that we could command in any adequate manner to communicate.

About three miles below Llangerig, in a southern direction, the river Darnel, which derives its source from the hills that bear its name, empties itself into the Wye. Pursuing

suing the course of the river, the Nanerth rocks in an extent of near three miles, form a beautiful screen to its northern bank.

On this spot the Wye, in an easy bend, gently rolls over its rugged bed, while the ascending road, girting the immense hills that are enriched with spreading oaks and luxuriant underwood, peculiarly invited the pencil: Through these, the rocks in various fantastic forms, perpetually break upon the eye, and the cottages interspersed among the distant hills, relieve the wide-spread and extended scenery. On the brow of a rising hill, in the fore ground, a group of cattle which covered it, seemed at the instant, as if placed there by design to complete the view. Beneath, the gentle river Marteg, the receptacle of many smaller streams that arise in the vicinity of Llanidlos, ripling over its pebbly bed, loses its name and its current in the broader channel of the Wye.

SECTION. II.

FROM Nanerth rocks, after a pleasant ride of about three miles on the bank of the Wye, we reached Rhaidr Gwy; the word Rhaidr signifies a cataract, or fall of water, and is frequently applied to those falls, among the mountains of Snowden in Carnarvonshire.

CAMDEN seems to think that from the word Rhaidr, the county of Radnor, through the west angle of which, this river directs its course derived its name. The bridge at Rhaidr consists of one wide arch, which from its base forms a very large segment of a circle. It is a plain structure and has little but its romantic accompaniments to recommend it; the immense pile of rocks on which it is elevated, carries the arch so high as to afford from beneath it, an extensive prospect of the adjoining country, in which a small Welsh building called Cwmtather Church appears in a whimsical point of view. The annexed sketch was taken from below the bridge, where the combination of objects is wonderfully grand; and in this dry season, displays in full force the ponderous rocky substances of which it is composed. But in consequence of this drought, we had the misfortune to lose the display and thunder of its cataract, which a less friendly state of the elements would have exhibited in all its grandeur. The stones over which the waters in this vicinity roll, are of an immense size, and in their forms, partake both of the majestic, and the grotesque; their diversified hues, and vast angular prominencies afford in certain lights and in some seasons of the day, under the rays of a bright sun the most brilliant and picturesque effect. Over the bridge passes the high road that leads to Aberystwyth,

ryftwith, and a more rugged and dreary path, is perhaps fcarce to be trod in any of the frequented parts of this principality. Rhaidr, though now but a miferable place, derived formerly fome confequence from its caftle, which was advantageoufly fituated in a nook of the river not far from the bridge, but of which no trace at prefent remains. Near the fpot whereon the caftle ftood is a deep trench cut out of a folid rock, and not far diftant, are feveral large Tumuli, or Barrows, called in Welfh, Kern, and Keido. Thefe are conjectured to have been raifed as memorials of the dead. Camden confirms this idea, and obferves, not very confiftently indeed with the refpect due to the memory of the departed, " that it is ftill the " cuftom to caft heaps of ftones on the " graves of malefactors and felf mur-
" derers."

At what period the caftle at Rhaidr was built

built is not ascertained, but it was repaired by Rhys Prince of South Wales in the reign of Richard the first, and near it says Camden, " is a vast wilderness rendered very
" dismal by many crooked ways and high
" mountains, into which as a proper place
" of refuge, that bane of his native country,
" King Vortigern, whose very memory the
" Britons curse, withdrew himself, when he
" had at last repented of his abominable
" wickedness, in calling in the English
" Saxons, and incestuously marrying his own
" daughter."

His address to the Barons, on the subject of calling in the aid of the Saxons, is thus recorded by an anonymous author.

" My Lords, vain compliment would suit but ill
" The present time, I therefore briefly thank you,
" But e'er we part, fain would I crave your hearing.
" Our Troops have now been long disus'd to War—
" Yet do not think I mean their fame to tarnish,
" O-

" Or on a Briton throw the damned flur
" Of shameful cowardice. No, my good Lords,—
" But though their ribs do serve as castle walls,
" And fast imprison their strong Lion hearts,
" Yet e'en the Lion, when full gorg'd with food
" Will bask and tamely lay him down to sleep—
" Then in such sort, hath undisturbed peace,
" And want of custom, (nature's substitute,
" That changes e'en our very properties)
" Soften'd their manhood. Then t'were policy
" That we should court the Saxons to our aid!
" This too will in our Britons raise the flame
" Of bright and generous emulation.
" Say Lords! doth this my proposition please you?

BELOW Rhaidr we soon lost sight of that immense rocky scenery, so eminently characterizing its neighborhood, and every reach of the river yielded additional richness and verdure. A detail of each minute change of prospect that occurs in a tour of this nature, however gratifying at the moment to the eye of the curious and picturesque traveller, would be tedious and uninteresting; it is therefore the business of description

tion to record only the moſt material objects as they occur, and leave imagination to paint the reſt. About three miles below Rhaidr, the Wye receives a confiderable ſupply of water from the rivers Eland and Clanven, which unite at a diſtance of about four miles from their conflux with our river. Below this a copious ſtream called the Ither, which in its courſe receives the Dulas and Comar, makes a confiderable addition to the waters of the Wye. From the brow of a hill about two miles before we reach the town of Builth, the ſcenery is peculiarly beautiful, the river ſpreads itſelf into a bay, and the immenſe rocky ſubſtances with which its bed has hitherto been ſpread, riſe here in various detached forms many yards above its ſurface, exhibiting ſo many ſmall iſlands, and agreeable breaks in the fore ground of the landſcape

The annexed view was ſketched from
this

this spot, in which it is much to be regretted that the bridge of Builth could not be introduced, as it would confiderably have added to the beauty of the fcenery. Builth is a town of little confequence, yet from its antiquity, and the falubrity of its air, it becomes highly deferving our attention. We happened to be there on a market day, when the town was fo thronged with people, that we could fcarcely pafs through it. It refembled rather a fair than a market, and the immenfe croud collected together, prefented to the eye a fcene in effect, fimilar to that of one continued mafs of long blue cloaks, apparently in perpetual motion. Not a houfe, nor a ftable but was occupied, and it was really a matter of aftonifhment, that in fo fmall a town, and on fo common an occafion as that of a weekly market, fuch a vaft concourfe of people fhould have been affembled; but a market or fair, is the pride and glory of the Welsh; and, happy fouls! why should they not in a sultry summer's day, enjoy the suffocating luxury of a long blue cloak, as well as the Londoner his summer theatre, amidst " the raging dog " star's heat."

In an extensive tour through Wales, I witnessed a scene at Aberystwith very similar to that I have just described, and as the surrounding objects were there more peculiarly marked with the picturesque than those at Builth, a representation of the scene, although at a considerable distance from hence, may perhaps not prove unacceptable to the reader. In this view appears part of the castellated dwelling of Uvedale Price, Esq; a man not less distinguished for the elegance with which he cultivates the fine arts, than for his powers of discrimination, and the accuracy with which he defines them.

The

The house is recently erected on the shore, and commands an extensive prospect of the sea, the only one in fact it does command.

At this market or fair, the usual artifices to amuse and delude, were exhibited with the usual success; other centuries revolve, and other generations arise, but rustic manners remain unchanged, the same pursuits occupy the mind, and the same toys interest and beguile. There were, " Ribbands of all the colors ith' rain-
" bow. Dancing and music, ballads all piti-
" ful and true, one of a fish that appeared
" upon the coast, on Wednesday the four-
" score of April, forty thousand fadom
" above water." Autolicus with all his rhetoric could not more artfully have displayed his wares, nor could the following lines have had a better effect on his auditors than the tricks presented here.

" Lawn

> "Lawn as white as driven snow,
> "Cyprus, black as e'er was crow;
> "Gloves as sweet as damask roses,
> "Masks for faces, and for noses;
> "Bugle bracelets, necklace amber,
> "Perfume for a lady's chamber;
> "Golden quoifs, and stomachers,
> "For my lads to give their dears;
> "Pins and poking-sticks of steel,
> "What maids lack from head to heal:
> "Come, buy of me, come: come, buy, come, buy,
> "Buy, lads, or else your lasses cry: come buy."

BUILTH is happily encompassed with a range of hills that afford shelter to the place, and screen the neighbouring woods with which it is enriched. On the skirt of the town stand the remains of an ancient castle; they comprise near four acres of ground, and though not sufficiently massed to form an object for the pencil, yet the remaining fragments convey a general idea of its former dignity.

THE eminence which is contiguous to the

the remains of the fortress, denotes what the Romans called the Presidium. This castle is reported to have been erected by the Breoses and Mortimers, after the demolition of a former one by Rhys ap Gryffydh. Ptolomy calls the town of Builth, Bullæum Silurum, from whence it derived its name, but Doctor Horsly is inclined to think that the ancient Bullæum of Antoninus, was at Uſke in Monmouthſhire, from the ruins of a Roman fort, or city, being found there. The neighbourhood of that place is ſtill called Bualht.

TRAVERSING the vicinity of the castle, our Welſh guide pointed out to us a field at about two miles diſtance, called Cavan, in which Prince Llewellyn is reported to have been buried, and ſo fertile he obſerved was the ſoil, that each ſtem bore two heads of corn.

From the same authority, we are told that as that Prince was one day crossing the field in disguise, he asked of an old woman the name of a small brook that ran across it, who replied, it was called Nantytrrad, then said he, let it in future be named Cwm Llewellyn, for that shall be the burial place of that Prince. Where is there a Welchmen who does not deplore the loss of his brave Llewellyn? but our guide drew much consolation from their being yet a good Prince of Wales, who in the hour of need, would certainly defend and fight for his countrymen. Llewellyn is reported to have been murthered in a small castle that stood at a place called Llechryd, about one mile from Builth, while he was meditating his escape into Glamorganshire. A modern house, with a moat surrounding it that includes about three acres, marks the spot whereon the castle stood. Builth Castle is well situated for defence, it stands on an eminence,

eminence, and the point of land, is in part furrounded by the beautiful river Irvon, which in a femicircular direction winds its courfe into the Wye, about half a mile above the town. This river is of confiderable width, and derives its fource from the hills in the vicinity of Strata Florida in the county of Cardigan; thence after taking a fouth weft direction it winds towards the north eaft, and falls into the Wye near Builth. Within a fmall diftance of its junction with our river, it receives a brook called the Wevery, which rifes on the Brecknockfhire hills abought eight miles diftant, and produces remarkable high flavoured falmon and trout.

NEAR to the Wye a new ftone bridge is building over the Irvon, contiguous to the old one which was of wood. This new ftructure confifts of fix eliptical arches; it is erecting at the joint expence of the counties

ties of Brecon and Radnor. The elevated span of the upper circle of this bridge, however neceſſary here from the great floods that happen in the winter ſeaſon, is yet a taſte too prevalent in the general conſtruction of our bridges. The bed of the upper ſurface is uſually ſo high as to become a large ſegment of a circle; this cuſtom militates not only againſt every principal of utility to the horſe and traveller, but ſhuts out the general proſpect, which even by an artiſt whoſe ideas are not too narrowly confined to his own ſcience, ſhould in a country like this be made an object of ſome conſideration.

In Italy and France, a contrary ſyſtem has very judiciouſly been adopted, by which means, in every point of view the eye finds relief from the diverſified ſcenery around. This practice is ſupported by the claſſical productions of the elegant Claude Lorraine, who, whether he deſigns from nature, or has

recourſe

recourse to his own refined ideas of his art, always adheres to this principle. Near Builth are the remains of Llandrindod-wells, once in high esteem, and celebrated for their excellent medicinal quality. This spring of water issues out of the side of a rock, which is of the slate kind, it is strongly impregnated with nitrous salt, sulphur, and steel; and produces an effect similar to the waters of Scarborough and Cheltenham, but it is of a more powerfully quality. The wells are now greatly in decay, and consequently are not so much frequented as formerly. On a high hill named Caven Durris, about a mile from Builth, David Thomas, Esq; has erected a handsome stone residence, which when viewed from the town, appears too much exposed, but on a near approach, is found to be happily screened from the northern winds by the surrounding hills: It command a very noble and extensive view, as well on its own level towards the South, as from that part which looks down towards the town of Builth, and at the same time includes a beautiful command of the meandering course of the rivers Wye and Irvon, and of the extensive bridge of Builth in the vale beneath. This bridge is a simple and well constructed modern edifice, consisting of six arches, within a mile of which a small river called the Dihono having a small bridge of one arch thrown over it, empties itself into the Wye. From the ferry a little below, a beautiful reach of the river terminates in a view of the small remains of Aberadway castle, of which no history is to be traced. Its ruin is very insignificant, little more than a stone wall, now ever grown with ivy remains. At the extremity of it are the fragments of two round towers. These rude specimens of art, are finely contrasted by the adjoining and truly wonderful productions of nature. These are an immense range of rocks running parrallel with the river, exhibiting a variety of the most

strange

strange and fantastic forms imaginable. In different points of view, they convey to the mind, the idea of so many towers and castles shooting from amidst the oak coppices and other shrubs that inrich this majestic scenery. These vast prominencies in their various shapes, received at the instant of viewing them, additional grandeur and effect from the solemn shade, produced by a declining sun, and presented a scene truly worthy the pencil of a Salvator, or amongst our countrymen, his rival, the late John Mortimer. Near this charming spot, the river Edwa, from which these rocks derive their name, empties itself into our river. For a considerable distance in passing down the Wye, we have on a smaller scale perpetual breaks of the same rocky kind of scenery till we reach Llangoed, the seat of Mr. Edwards; from hence we ride through a charming wood of young oaks, ranged for a considerable distance on an elevated bank

bank of the Wye, they give at each break and opening, an enchanting view of our beautiful and picturesque river, which on the approach to a village called Swains, about a mile distant, wears the appearance of an extensive bay, while the mountains in the back ground gradually recede, and the general face of the landscape assumes a new character. In the annexed view of Glasebury, the scene when contrasted with that at Aberedway or at Builth, will best illustrate this idea, here all around wears an air of placidity; the river's rocky bed no more agitates the water in its course, it flows a tranquil and a gentle stream, reflected on whose glassy surface under the evening's lengthening shade

" Down bend its banks, the trees depending grow;
" And skies beneath with answ'ring colors glow.

In the midst of this rich and beautiful valley, an elegant stone bridge of seven arches

arches is thrown acrofs the river. It was built about fourteen years ago by the family of Edwards, under the direction of their father, the celebrated architect of Pont-y-pridd. The adjoining view was made in Auguſt, 1794; in the enſuing winter the bridge was totally deſtroyed, which will in in ſome degree give value to this ſketch, as a memorial of that which is at preſent, little more than a wreck; every arch of it having been blown up by the torrent of ice, which poured down on the very ſudden thaw, after the long froſt in the begining of 1795.

SECTION III.

ON our approach to the town of Hay, we pass its small church, situated on a high and clayey bank of the river, from whence the town and adjoining objects, afford little worthy the attention of the artist. To preface this section, I have therefore selected a general view of the town and surrounding country, from a spot about a mile below the bridge, which presents a scene highly enriched by an assemblage of woods, meadows, and corn fields, at once extensive, and in a peculiar degree interesting.

THE town is happily situated on the declivity of a hill, on which the houses rising gradually, convey the idea of a place of infinitely more consequence than really it possesses, and in no small degree gives the general

neral outline of an Italian landscape. The face of this scenery and bridge is fully illustrative of the position laid down in the last section, of the superior beauty of flat bridges over those that are elevated. This bridge is formed of seven arches and in the year 1795, met with a similar fate to the preceding one, and which were thrown across the torrents that pour themselves along the vallies of this mountainous country.

THE purple hue of the distance called the black mountains, affords a good background to this scenery, which is heightened by the rich glow of a noon-tide sun, darting at the instant, and giving force and relief to every object. These mountains extend fourteen or fifteen miles towards a place called Monmouth Cap, about eight miles from Abergavenny. The head of water in the fore groud of the view, is formed from a small river called Boonewayne Brook,

Brook, which supplies the neigbouring mill with water; the goat who stood browsing on a high bank of the river before us, was an object we were not accustomed to meet, with even in Wales, as I do not remember to have seen more than three, in the course of a long tour through this country.

THE town of Hay was formerly called Hain, it derives its name from the British word Tregelhi, which, says Camben " may
" be rendered Hasely, or Hasleton; it ap-
" pears to have been well known to the
" Romans, some remains of their walls
" being still visible, and many of their coins
" having been found here." He likewise says " the ancient town was consumed
" by fire by the profligate rebel, Owen
" Glyndwr or Glendower, in his marches
" through this country." Our divine bard has put the following lines into the mouth

of Glendower, when speaking of his antagonist.

" Three times hath *Henry Bolingbroke* made head
" Against my pow'r, thrice from the banks of *Wye*,
" And sandy-bottom'd *Severn*, have I sent
" Him bootless home, and weather-beaten back."

THIS place anciently belonged to William de Brus, Lord of Brecknock, and was nearly destroyed by Lewis, Dauphin of France, in 1216, who had been invited into England by the Barons disaffected to King John.

THE town of Hay is situated on the extreme angle of Brecknockshire, and on the borders of Herefordshire. Near the church, on the highest land on the brink of the river, there anciently stood a castle built by the Normans, of which little more now remains than a mound of earth, and the entrenchtrenchments that surround it. The present castle stands nearly in the centre of the town. Its Gothic entrance, and the Ivy over-growing the remains of the ancient tower, produce a striking effect on the approach to this venerable ruin.

A LARGE house adjoining, is the property of Richard Wellington, Esq; It is erected on the site of the old castle, and appears to have been the work of the age of James I. Within a few years, it has been modernized, by which it has in some degree been stripped of that small share of the picturesque, that in some instances is to be found even in that barbarous age of architecture. As the castle is not generally noticed by the traveller, nor has any print that I can learn, ever yet been given of it, the annexed view may not prove unacceptable to the curious enquirer. On quitting Hay, the Wye receives a considerable body of

water

water from the river Dulas, across which is a stone bridge of one arch. Thus assisted, our river becomes a copious stream, and has been long rendered navigable in the winter seasons. For this purpose two statutes were passed in parliament, the one in the fourteenth of Charles II. the other in the seventh of William III.

About two miles below the town, the ruin of the once famous Clifford castle presents itself; it stands on a considerable eminence on the bank of the Wye, is well situated for defence, and forms a boundary to the western part of the county of Hereford. Its walls are not sufficiently high, nor are the parts so broken and irregular as to afford a complete picturesque object, but it has yet considerable attractions to merit the notice of the speculative and inquisitive traveller. Camden says, that it is recorded in doom's-day book, to have been built by William Fitzosborn,

Fitzosborn, Earl of Hereford. It came afterwards to Walter, the son of Richard de Ponts, a Norman, who came into England with William the Conqueror, Walter took his name of De Clifford from this castle, and from him descended the illustrious family of the earls of Cumberland. We shall not enter into a detail of the warlike exploits performed in this place, but confine ourselves to the well known story of fair Rosamond, daughter of an earl of Clifford, who was born in this castle. The story, whether fabulous or true, has been deemed not unworthy the attention, both of the poet and historian. Master Hollinshead in his usual quaintness of style, thus speaks of King Henry the second's incontinence, and of his particular attachment to the fair Rosamond, " for not contented with the
" use of his wife, he kept many concubines,
" but namely he delited most in the com-
" panie

" panie of a pleafant damofell, whome he
" 'cleped the rofe of the world, the common
" people named hir *Rofamond*, for hir paffing
" beautie, properneffe of perfon, and plea-
" fant wit, with other amyable qualities,
" being verily a rare and peereleffe peece in
" thofe days. He made for hir an houfe
" at Woodftocke in Oxfordfhire, like to a
" laberinth, that is to meane, wrought like
" a knot in a garden, called a maze, with
" fuch turnings and windings in and out,
" that no creature might finde her nor
" come to hir, except he were inftructed by
" the king, or fuch as were fecrete with him
" in that matter. But the common report
" of the people is, that the queene finally
" found her out by a filke thread, whiche
" the king had drawne forth of hir chamber
" with his foote, and dealte with hir in fuch
" fharpe and cruell wife, that fhe lyved not
" long after. She was buried in the Nun-
                                    " rie

" rie of Godſtow beſide Oxforde, with theſe
" verſes upon hir tumbe."

" Hic jacet in tumulo, Roſamundi non Roſamunda,
" Non redolet ſed olet, quæ redolere ſolet."

We cannot quit this ſubject, the family of the De Cliffords, without adverting to another of its noble deſcendants, George Clifford, the third earl of Cumberland, who in 1525, was advanced to the dignity of an earl. The feats of this adventurous and renowned warrior, are tranſmitted to us by various hiſtorians, and though to many perſons they may be well known, yet ſome mention of him in this place, may not be thought irrelevant to our ſubject. This nobleman was one of the peers who ſat in judgment on Mary Queen of Scots, and became afterwards a great favourite of her couſin Elizabeth.

beth. He signalized himself highly at sea in various engagements against the Spaniards, and behaved with much intrepidity during the memorable encounter with the invincible Armada. In consequence of his gallantry the Queen created him an Admiral, and a few years after, a Knight of the Garter; he was likewise one of the lords sent out with the forces to reduce the Earl of Essex. He died in London at the Savoy, at the age of forty seven, in the year 1605.

We cannot pass over a striking instance of gallantry, in this extraordinary hero, as recorded by Mr. Pennant, which appears fully to keep pace with his bravery as a naval commander. " At an audience, " which the earl had after one of his " expeditions, Queen Elizabeth, perhaps " designedly, dropped one of her gloves.

His

" His lordship took it up, and presented it
" to her; upon which she graciously de-
" sired him to keep it as a mark of her
" esteem. He adorned the glove with dia-
" monds, and wore it in the front of his
" high crowned hat on days of tour-
" nament." This circumstance is recorded
in a very curious and rare print of the earl,
engraved by Robert White, in which the
glove appears. Another instance of the
queen's favor to this earl of Cumberland,
was, her appointing him her champion in
her tilting matches, in which exercise he
excelled all the nobility of his time. His
magnificent armour worn in this age of chi-
valry, was adorned with roses and fleur de
lis, and is now preserved at Appleby Castle
in Westmoreland. He married Margaret,
third daughter of Francis earl of Bedford,
by whom he had three children, two sons
who died young, and a daughter named
Anne,

Anne, who was succeffively married to Richard earl of Dorset, and to Philip earl of Pembroke and Montgomery.

This lady appears by the following letter to have inherited with the family eftates, all the bravery and spirit of her great anceftors. Sir Joseph Williamfon, when secretary of ftate to Charles the II. wrote to the Countefs, wifhing to name a candidate to her for the borough of Appleby, to which fhe returned the following fpirited anfwer "I have been bullied by an " ufurper, I have been neglected by a court, " but I will not be dictated to by a fubject. " Your man fhan't ftand."

"ANNE, DORSET;

" Pembroke and Montgomery."

Dr. Campbell, in his Philosophy of Rhetoric, highly commends the expression of this letter, he says, " an ordinary spirit " would have employed as many pages to " express the same thing, as there are af- " firmations in this short letter." Of this extraordinary lady, Dr. Donne remarked, " that in her younger years, she knew well " how to discourse of all things, from pre- " destination, to flea-silk."

From this digression, which we hope will not prove uninteresting, we return again to the main subject of our enquiry.

The winding and mazy course of the Wye in about two miles, brings us to Whitney, where, in 1794, the piers and part of the arches of a new stone bridge were in great forwardness, but in the suc- ceeding spring, the whole was swept away by by that sudden thaw and torrent, whose devastations we have more than once had occasion to notice. In this unfinished state, the busy scenery of the various artificers at work, a ferry boat perpetually in motion, and the distant village church, peeping above the hills in the back ground, produced altogether a subject well worthy the pencil; but from the confined nature of this work, and the abundant rich, and luxuriant scenery, we have yet to display, we feel it impossible to insert every object in picture, however highly it may merit our notice in description. Passing several beautiful villages, we reach Willersley, in the vicinity of which, the extensive range of Merbidge Hills afforded us, from their summit, a grand and extensive view of the surrounding country. Another noble object presents itself in this neighbourhood, which bears the name of Brobery's Scar: its principal attractions are the bold and majestic

jeſtic roughneſſes of its form, that contraſt beautifully with the views, more immediately upon the eye, on the bank of our river. Hence, amidſt a profuſion of rich and beautiful ſcenery, at a place called Rhydſpence, the river quits Radnorſhire, and glides its eaſy courſe towards Bradwardin. This town ſtands on an eaſy aſcent on the bank of the Wye, and preſents itſelf in a happy point of view above the bridge, the northern bank of the river riſes to a conſiderable height, and is richly cloathed with ſhrubbery. In the annexed view we have aimed at a repreſentation of this beautiful and romantic ſcene. The river here acquires a conſiderable width, and though in a dry ſeaſon, has a proportionable depth of water. In this vicinity there was formerly a caſtle, of which very little remains. This place gave birth, and name to the famous Thomas Bradwardin, Archbiſhop of Canterbury, who,

who, from his variety of knowledge and proficiency in the abstruse branches of learning, obtained his title of Doctor Profundus. Below this village we glided down this deep and majestic stream, amidst a rich and fertile country, till we reached Mocca's Court, the seat of Sir George Cornwall, Bart. It is pleasantly situated on an eminence, on the southern bank of the Wye, within a spacious park, and commands a full and extensive view of the beautiful meanderings of the river.

This place was anciently called Moches, and formed a part of the possessions of St. Guthlach, in the City of Hereford. The ancient house stood below the site of the present, which is a modern structure, and was in part built from the ruin of Bredwardin Castle. In descending towards Hereford we passed a variety of elegant villas,

villas, rich in fituation, and very happily felected as fummer refidences; amongft thefe Belmont, the feat of Dr. Matthews, is peculiarly worthy of attention. The views from hence, in each direction of the river, are highly attractive, and art and nature under the guidance of tafte, are happily combined to produce a rich and beautiful effect.

SECTION. IV.

THIS view of the ancient bridge and venerable cathedral of Hereford, affords the moſt picturesque, and ſtriking combination of objects, that came within our obſervation. The bridge is of ſtone, and confiſts of eight Gothic arches, it is evidently of great antiquity, but at what period it was built, hiſtory affords little information on which we can rely. Leland conjectures that it was erected about the ſame time with the caſtle, that is, ſoon after the conqueſt.

THE preſent beautiful cathedral, ſays Camden, " was founded by biſhop Reinelm, " in 1079, in the reign of Henry I. and by " his ſucceſſors was enlarged, by adding to it " a neat college and fine houſes for the pre- " bendaries." The Biſhop, he likewiſe ſays,

" has

"has three hundred and two churches in his diocese." The revenues of the bishopric were valued, in the 26th of Henry VIII. at eight hundred and thirty one pounds fourteen shillings and a penny. The present venerable structure has undergone many changes, and has been greatly encreased and beautified by several of its bishops since its first erection, a circumstance that naturally followed from the immense expense attending such an undertaking, which must at any period have greatly exceeded the income, even of the wealthiest abbot or bishop that the church has yet known. The similarity of parts in the style of its architecture, has induced some persons to conjecture that it was all built at the same period: this I judge could not have been the case, there is more reason to believe that the earliest forms served as a model for future ages to work upon. It has undergone shameful depredations: the chief of which were occasioned by the puritanical
principles

principles of the laſt century, when a blind zeal upon religious ſubjects devoted the moſt beautiful and venerable veſtiges of antiquity to ruin and deſtruction, as abominations hateful in the eyes of God and man. The form of the arches ſeems to indicate that the earlier part of this building was erected about the æra of the Saxon architecture; its columns are peculiarly ponderous and maſſive, they appear to have been erected " not for an age, but for all " time." Some monuments of their biſhops ſtill remain, amongſt which, in the north wing is the ſhrine of biſhop Cantilupe. The monument of the family of the Bohuns, in the library is curious, and deſerves the attention of the antiquary: a recumbent figure is laying beneath a pointed Gothic arch, round which are a number of hogs, covered with a kind of body cloth, on which are painted the arms of the family, each hog having before him an apple to which

which he seems smelling. This ancient family of the Bohuns and the Lacies earls of Hereford, are said by some writers to have been the founders of Hereford castle, which Leland asserts " to have been one of the " fairest, largest, and strongest in England." The preceding view of Hereford was made in the summer of 1794, at which time the tower of the cathedral was surrounded with a scaffold, and the whole of the building under a thorough repair, from the dreadful accident that happened in the year 1786: On the 17th day of April in that year, about half past six in the evening, the west tower of the cathedral with part of the body of the church unfortunately fell down. The above accident did not happen without giving evident signs of gradual decay, both from the dropping of many stones, and the settling of the arches, which had been remarked for two or three years previous to the event. This dreadful catastrophe

trophe was sufficiently foreseen to prevent any fatal consequences. No lives were lost though many persons were passing the church yard at the time, and we of this day have the less reason to deplore the accident, as the rulers of this church, have had the good sense to make use of the rare talents of an architect, whose knowledge of the Gothic, and natural taste for grandeur and simplicity, so peculiarly fitted him for the office of restoring this venerable fabric to its true characteristical dignity, and who does not appear to have deviated from the original design, where it was possible to conform to it. One principal improvement has been the removing some walls that encircled a material part of the church, by which means a view was opened, of two beautiful chapels, called Stanbury and Audley, that had been long concealed from the public eye.

Mr. Wyat's estimate of the repair of this

this building was seven thousand pounds, five thousand of which was raised by subscription. But I am imformed that to complete this repair, the whole expense will amount to at least thirteen thousand pounds.

This magnificent structure has ever been considered by the antiquary, notwithstanding its irregularity, as a splendid specimen of the piety and munificence of our early churchmen; and the arched roof of the upper cross aisle, supported by a single pillar, is peculiarly deserving attention. Tradition says, it was erected in the reign of William Rufus, by Robert de Lozinga, second bishop of the see of Hereford. The height of the tower was one hundred and twenty-five feet, upon which was a lofty spire, that has, since the accident, been taken down.

On the site on which this cathedral stands there was anciently a church, founded during

during the zenith of the Saxon heptarchy about the ninth century, soon after which it became a cathedral, and Hereford was made the see of a bishop. The cathedral was destroyed, and the city sacked in the reign of Edward the Confessor, by Griffin prince of South Wales who made the bishop prisoner. At the Norman invasion the city was in ruins, and within its walls and the suburbs, there were not, according to doomsday book, more than one hundred and three men.

At a small distance from the cathedral stands the vicar's college, it forms a square, within which is a plain but venerable cloister. From its elevated situation, it commands a beautiful view of the meandering course of our river Wye, and its fertile and verdant banks. Although it is not the professed intention of this work to enter into a minute history of cities, or towns, yet the antiquity

quity of this venerable place demands our attention, and cannot be paſſed over in ſilence, we ſhall therfore mention the once elegant building of the chapter houſe, of which, though but a ſmall fragment preſents itſelf, there is yet ſufficient of the picturesque to attract the notice of the curious traveller, nor can the remains of the Black Fryers with its beautiful croſs, or rather ſtone pulpit, be paſſed unnoticed, the latter is here preſerved in a wood cut from a ſketch made on the ſpot in 1794.

The building is Hexagonal, open at every fide, and round it is a flight of fix fteps. The fhaft of the crofs which is broken off, refts on a table of the fame form in the centre of the building, and fpreads itfelf towards the roof in ramifications that produce a very beautiful effect. Some of the embattlements yet remain on the upper part of the building, the whole of which appears to have been finifhed with great care and elegance. From this building, fermons were delivered by the fryers, who were then extremely popular, to the multitude who were fheltered under the cloifter, that it is prefumed, furrounded this building. An hofpital in 1614, was founded on the fite whereon ftood the black fryars, by Sir Thomas Coningfby of Hampton Court, in this county, who was then proprietor of the ruins, and by him it was endowed with confiderable eftates in Leicefterfhire, and

was

was intended as a relief to the worn out soldier and superannuated faithful servant.

THE city of Hereford, appears by its remaining walls, to have been well and regularly fortified, and its castle must have been a very capital fortress. The site whereon it stood retains the name of Castle Green, and affords a pleasant retreat, commanding a very beautiful view of the river beneath and of the surrounding country. This being a remarkable dry season, barges have been laying at Hereford for upwards four months, for want of water to carry them down.

THE principal articles of navigation are timber, bark, and grain, and the back carriage, is coals from Ledbrook and other places below Ross. Hereford is not favourably situated for manufactures or commerce. It is ill supplied with fuel, and that not good,

good, and the uncertain ftate of the river, from its fhoals and great rapidity, prevents that conftant and uniform navigation which can alone fupport a regular and extenfive trade. To remove thefe barriers, feveral attempts, I am informed, have been made, but the eftimate of expenfes has been fo enormous, that the meafure has always proved abortive.

Quitting Hereford, the Wye bends its courfe round a point of land for a diftance of near two miles, when we are again brought almoft as near to the town, as when we quitted it. The river as we paffed down, ftill continued its circuitous windings, but with a more placid furface, feldom meeting any obftruction in its courfe, from thofe rocky fubftances that formed the grand characteriftic of the ftream in its earlier ftages. The general face of the country is rich in verdure, and the cattle grazing on the banks of the river or laving in its ?rear?, are objects that perpetually contribute to enliven the scene.

About six miles below Hereford, the Wye receives the river Lug, one of the three principal rivers in this county; it derives its source from the mountains in the north east part of Radnorshire, and running east, through Herefordshire to Leominster, takes a south east direction towards the Wye; in its course it is joined by several smaller streams, and on its near approach to our river, becomes a stream of considerable magnitude. About a mile from the bank of the Wye, this river runs through the pleasant village of Mordiford, and adds much to the picturesque scenery of the place. On the east end of the church of Mordiford is represented in plaster, an enormous dragon or serpent, the history of which

which is thus recorded. Some centuries ago, we know not when, a dragon is reported to have been the devourer of all the cattle on the adjoining hills called Offwood, and was a monster of such terrific qualities, that no one could for a great length of time, be found bold enough to undertake his destruction, till at length a pardon being granted to a condemned criminal, on condition that he would undertake it, he atchieved his purpose, by flaying the dragon as he was solacing himself in a cyder hogshead. This wonderful relation, seems to be generally credited by the people in the neighbourhood, as no doubt it was at the building of this edifice, or this strange monster would not have been represented in so terrific a form, and in so conspicuous a place as the front of the church. After relating this wonderful circumstance, may we be permitted to quote another, not less so from the learned Camden. He says, that " near the conflux of
" the

"the Lug and the Wye, eastward, a hill
"which they call Marcley hill, did in the
"year 1575, rouse itself as it were out of
"sleep, and for three days together, shoving
"its prodigious body forward with a hor-
"rible roaring noise, and overturning every
"thing in its way, raised itself (to the
"great astonishment of the beholders) to a
"higher place; by that kind of earthquake,
"I suppose, which the Naturalists call Bras-
"matia." On a hill adjoining the village, a large stone house has been recently erected by a Mr. Hereford, which deserves notice from the extensive and beautiful view it commands of Hereford and the surrounding country.

ABOUT a mile below Mordiford, we pass a large brick mansion belonging to the Duke of Norfolk, called Holme Lacy, formerly the seat of the ancient family of the Scudamores. On this site stood an abbey for

for Premonstratensian cannons, dedicated to the Virgin Mary and Thomas a Becket, founded by William Fitzwain in the beginning of the reign of Henry the third; the house is a flat uninteresting building, but comprises within its view a beautiful and picturesque prospect on the opposite side of the river, called Fownhope. The village is situated amidst a rich thicket of verdant and woody scenery, on an extensive slope rising from a rocky bank of the Wye.

This richly diversified hill, is at a proper distance from the eye, to enable it distinctly to mark the several species of trees of which it is composed; these cannot be more aptly described, than in the lines of Dyer, on a similar subject, in his charming poem of Grongar Hill.

"The

" The gloomy pine, the poplar blue,
" The yellow beech, the fable yew,
" The flender fir, that taper grows,
" The fturdy oak, with broad fpread boughs."

AMONST the few houfes that are fcattered on this beautiful fcene, the principal are thofe of Mr. Lechmere, and Mr. Purchafe, who has a confiderable brewery here. A little below the next bend of the river, a range of hills called Capler hills, form a rich fcreen to the northern bank of the Wye. Thefe hills are upwards of a mile and a half in length, and are principally covered with oak trees, the foil which is of a reddifh caft, frequently breaks through the verdure of its plantations, and gives a warm and animated tinge to the landfcape. A high road paffes the fummit of thefe hills, that commands a beautiful profpect of the furrounding country, and the meandering river beneath. Near Brookhampton on Capler hill, is the remain of a very large fquare camp,

camp called Wobury, it appears to be double trenched, but narrow and near half a mile in length. About five years ago, near three acres of thefe hills fell into the Wye and narrowed its courfe, but it has from that circumſtance, obtained a more confiderable depth than we have before witneſſed in this river, being now in a dry feafon, upwards of five feet deep.

On the left of the river, at Aramſtone, is a fine view of the village of King's Caple fituated amidſt a beautiful aſſemblage of woods. Below this fpot on the oppofite bank is Harewood, the refidence of the Hofkins's an ancient family in the county of Hereford. This place is peculiarly worthy notice, as it compoſed part of the foreſt of Harewood, in which Ethelwold, king Edgar's miniſter had a caſtle. Here Mafon fixed the fcene, for his dramatic poem of Elfrida, and thus he defcribes the fcene before us

I " How

"How nobly does this venerable wood,
"Gilt with the glories of the orient sun
"Embosom yon fair mansion! the soft air
"Salutes me with most cool and temp'rate breath;
"And as I tread, the flow'r besprinkled lawn
"Sends up a gale of fragrance. I should guess,
"If e'er content deign'd visit mortal clime,
"This was her place of dearest residence."

From hence amidst a rich and woody country, admitting from its sameness little variety worthy either the pen or pencil, we pursued our course down the gentle stream till we reached the pleasant village of Selleck; its church is of a singular construction, and no less so is that of an epitaph I copied in the church yard, on the tombstone of one Richard Addis who died in 1788, aged 80.

"When Christ come riding on the clouds
"To view the world abroad,
"Angels and saints crying aloud
"Rise dead and meet the Lord:"

On the opposite side of the river, a
little

little below Harewood, is a fine grove of trees called Capie Tump, where an annual festival is held from all the neighbouring towns, and where

> " All the village train, from labor free,
> " Lead up their sports beneath the spreading tree."

About two miles below Selleck, we were gratified with the most beautiful and luxuriant view of Rofs, that I believe the country from any point affords.

SECTION V.

ON the approach to Rofs, a fine amphitheatre of trees called Afhwood, fkirts the fouthern bank of the Wye. From this charming fpot, near three miles above Rofs, The annexed view which comprehends the principal objects that compofe the beautiful in picturefque lan fcape was fketched. The town is fituated on the declivity of a hill at a happy diftance, and not too obtrufive on the eye; the rifing hills with which it is fcreened give a boldnefs of character to the fituation, nor is the winding of the river, and verdure of the country that enrich its banks, lefs charactereftic of this delightful neighbourhood. The hill to the right of the town is called the Chafe, and that on the left, Penyard-wood, on which formerly ftood a caftle, faid to have been deftroyed in the civil

civil wars. The white spire of Rofs church " bosomed high in tufted trees" has at this distance an effect peculiarly pleasing, but on a nearer approach, the town obtrudes too much on the eye, and the picturesque and beautiful, gradually disappear.

Rofs, abstracted from its elevated and delightful situation, has little to render it worthy attention; the prospect from the church yard a spot to which the traveller is generally conducted on his arrival, displays a very extensive and inchanting landscape both above and below the town.

The beautiful and meandering course of the river beneath, enriched with pleasure boats constantly in motion, in their passage to and from Chepstow, gives life and beauty to the scene. These boats are lightly constructed and are navigated by three men, either

ther with or without a fail. The heavy mafs of building called the Town Hall, from its general appearance conveys a faint idea of the worſt ſtyle of Saxon architecture; it is a ponderous and unmeaning heap of ſtone, huddled together in the taſteleſs reign of James the firſt, by one John Abel who erected a ſimilar building at Hereford; they vie with each other in want of taſte, and have nothing to render them worthy notice but their abſurdity, which I believe is not to be equalled by the dulleſt architect of that or any other period. At one end of the building, intended I preſume as an ornament, there is a noſeleſs buſt, ſuppoſed to be that of the merry monarch Charles the ſecond. In ſuch a ſtate of decay is the ſtone of which this edifice is compoſed, together with the heavy ſtyle of its architecture, that it has every appearance of having been erected as far back as the time of the Saxons.

Notwithstanding the disadvantage under which this building labors, I have yet considered the general view of which it forms a part as not devoid of interest, it comprizes the house in which the man of Ross resided till his death, now known by the sign of the King's Arm Inn. As every the most trifling circumstance relative to a character so highly distinguished by the pen of Pope, and still more highly dignified by the general voice of the people of Ross becomes interesting, I have here thought fit to give a view of the house in which he resided, and the adjoining buildings.

To the benevolent John Kyrle, a name almost lost in the superior title of the Good Man of Ross this town owes most of its improvements and charitable institutions.

He was born at Whitehouse, in the parish

S. Ireland del.

parish of Dymock, in the county of Hereford in 1637, served the office of sheriff for the county in 1683, and died in 1724.

From an income of only five hundred pounds a year, this good man appears to have derived every happiness to himself and to have diffused it with uncommon benevolence to all around him. This exemplary character has been so interestingly delineated by the pen of Pope, that the introduction of the following lines although well known, will need no apology for their insertion in this work.

" Rise honest muse! and sing the *Man of Ross*:
" Pleas'd Vaga echoes thro' her winding bounds,
" And rapid Severn hoarse applause resounds.
" Who hung with woods yon mountain's sultry brow?
" From the dry rock, who bade the waters flow?
" Not to the skies in useless columns tost,
" Or in proud falls magnificently lost,
" But clear, and artless, pouring thro' the plain
" Health to the sick, and solace to the swain.

K " Whose

"Whose cause-way parts the vale with shady rows?
"Whose seats the weary traveller repose?
"Who taught the heaven directed spire to rise?
"The *Man of Ross*, each lisping babe replies.
"Behold the market-place with poor o'erspread!
"*The Man of Ross* divides the weekly bread;
"He feeds yon alms-house, neat, but void of state,
"Where age, and want sit smiling at the gate;
"Him portion'd maids, apprentic'd orphans blest,
"The young who labor, and the old who rest.
"Is any sick? the *Man of Ross* relieves,
"Prescribes, attends, the medicine makes, and gives."
"Is there a variance? enter but his door,
"Balk'd are the courts, and contest is no more.
"Despairing Quacks with curses fled the place,
"And vile Attorneys, now an useless race.

B. "Thrice happy man! enabled to pursue
"What all so wish, but want the power to do!
"Oh say, what sums that gen'rous hand supply?
"What mines to swell that boundless charity?

P. "Of debts and taxes, wife and children clear,
"This man possest—five hundred pounds a year.
"Blush, grandeur, blush! proud courts withdraw your blaze,
"Ye little stars! hide your diminished rays.

B. "And what? no monument, inscription, stone?
"His race, his form, his name almost unknown?

P. "Who builds a church to God, and not to fame,
"Will never mark the marble with his name:

"Go,

"Go, search it there, where to be born and die,
"Of rich and poor makes all the history;
"Enough that virtue fill'd the space between
"Prov'd by the ends of being, to have been."

THE allusion of the poet, to a neglect in not raising a monument to the good man's name, no longer exists, for in 1776 a neat mural tablet was erected to his memory in the chancel of the church, by Colonel Money, to defray the expence of which, the sum of three hundred pounds was bequeathed by a Lady Kinnoul, whose property devolving to the Colonel, the good intention of the lady was by him accomplished. On this tablet the following lines are inscribed.

"THIS monument was erected in me-
"mory of Mr. John Kyrle, commonly cal-
"led the Man of Ross."

IT is somewhat singular that neither his age, nor the time of his death, are here men-

mentioned. The design for the monument was made by a Mr. Marsh of this town, who has introduced a bust of the good man that bears little resemblance to either of the two portraits I met with in Ross; one of these is in the possession of Philip Jones Esq; a gentleman, who by marriage with a descendant of John Kyrle, enjoys all his property, and by his urbanity renders himself a worthy representative of that exemplary character. This picture appears to be that of a person about thirty six years of age, and is evidently the work of Sir Peter Lely. The other portrait was at the King's Arms Inn, formerly the residence of John Kyrle, as described in the view given in this section, it represents him at a more advanced period of life, and on that account, although ill painted, it was preferred to the former as he is exhibited nearer the close of a life, long and happily spent in the promotion of virtue, and to the honor of human nature.

JOHN KYRLE,

Commonly called the Man of Ross.

Pub. for S. Ireland Mar. 1. 1797.

nature. I flatter myself the annexed etching from this picture will not prove unacceptable to the admirer and collector of portraits, as I do not remember to have ever seen a print of this exalted character. The original is said to have been sketched from the life unknown to Mr. Kyrle, on a sunday whilst he was attending divine service. He had often been solicited to sit for his picture, but no inducement could prevail on him to comply with the request of his friends.

It is reported of Mr. Kyrle, that his ordinary mode of dress, was very plain, and so mean as even to suggest the idea of indigence and want. And even more unfavourable conclusions have been made, from his general appearance, for upon no better foundation, it is said that when travelling in Oxfordshire on horseback, he was apprehended near Benson, upon a suspicion of having

having committed a robbery in a neighbouring county. I need not add that this charge was dismissed the instant his name was made known to the magistracy.

We cannot quit this town without noticing to the picturesque traveller, a charming walk made by Mr. Kyrle, which led to what he called his farm, it commands a beautiful view of the devious windings of the river beneath, and Wilton castle, bridge, &c. on the opposite shore.

SECTION VI.

ABOUT a mile below Rofs, Wilton Caftle firft attracts our attention. This ruin is fituated on the margin of the Wye, and affords with its furrounding objects in many points of view, fcenes not unworthy the attention of the antiquary or admirer of picturefque objects. Its weftern walls and round towers are in the moft perfect ftate of prefervation, but the annexed view, comprifing a part of the bridge, is felected as moft appropriate to the defign of this work and to exemplify the courfe of the river. The caftle has formerly covered a confiderable extent of ground, the greater part of which is now ufed as a garden. Camden fays " that king John gave Wilton with " the caftle to Henry Longchamp and that

it

" it came by marriage to William Fitz-
" hugh, and not long after, in King Ed-
" ward the firſt's time, to Reginald Grey,
" Juſtice of Cheſter, from whom by a long
" deſcent it came to Lord Grey of Wilton,
" whoſe ſon Arthur Lord Grey was Lord
" Deputy of Ireland." This noble perſon merits particular attention, as having been the early patron of our Spencer the poet, who accompanied him to Ireland as his ſecretary.

In the county of Cork, at a place called Kilcolman, Spencer is reported to have finiſhed his excellent poem of the Fairy Queen. The River Mulla, ſo often mentioned by him, ran through the grounds of the houſe in which he reſided. His gratitude to his patron is thus recorded, in a ſonnet addreſſed to him, and is prefixed to the poem.

" Moſt

" Moſt noble lord the pillor of my life,
" And patrone of my muſes pupillage:
" Through whoſe large bountie, poured on me rife
" In the firſt ſeaſon of my feeble age,
" I nowe doe live bound yours by vaſſalage;" &c.

At what period Wilton Caſtle went out of the family of the Greys is not mentioned, but it afterwards belonged to the Lord Chandos, from whom it deſcended to the duke of Chandos who built Canons in Middleſex. The remains of this caſtle, with Aconbury, Dewſall, and other conſiderable eſtates in the neighbourhood bolonging to this family, amounting to near four thouſand pounds per annum, were ſold ſome years ago to the governors of Guy's Hoſpital. The caſtle is reported to have been principally deſtroyed by fire, but at what period is not aſcertained. In ſupport of this idea we obſerved, that towards the ends of the timbers, many of them appeared to have
been

been much burned. On this spot an assemblage of rich and woody scenery, forms the leading feature of the vicinity of our river, and about two miles below Wilton bridge I would advise the admirer of the truly grand in landscape, to ascend the hill in the high road to Monmouth, where at a place called Pencreek, the eye is feasted with one of the most magnificent views this river affords. The distant church of Rofs, its neighboring woods and hills, and the meandering course of the Wye, all combine from hence to form this facinating scene. Here the course of the river is peculiarly marked, its channel is nobly formed, and wears a grandeur not to be met with in any other river we have yet seen in this country.

AMIDST a variety of enchanting views, passing from one bend of the river to another, Goodrich castle, on the summit of a
bold

bold promontary, amidſt an elegant woodland ſcene, nobly raiſes its ruined battlements, as if frowning on the ſtream beneath.

On aſcending the hill to contemplate the ſpoils of Time, who ravages alike the forms of beauty and the tower of ſtrength, by leaving for a moment the ordinary path and paſſing up what is called Conduit hill, Walford church, Roſs, and the ſurrounding country, at a happy diſtance, combine to form a landſcape of peculiar richneſs and beauty. Hiſtory does not inform us at what period this caſtle was erected, but we find that early as the fifth year of the reign of King John, William Marſhall, Earl of Pembroke had a grant of it. From this family it came to Talbot, Earl of Shrewſbury, in the reign of Edward the third, and in the twentieth year of Richard the ſecond, Sir John Scudamore of Holme Lacy was conſtituted its conſtable, during the minority

ority of John Lord Talbot, in whose family it continued till the fourteenth of James the First; at which period Gilbert Talbot, Earl of Shrewsbury died, leaving three daughters his coheiresses. Elizabeth the second daughter was married to Henry de Grey, Earl of Kent, by which marriage he became possessor of this manor, which continued in the family till the death of Henry Duke of Kent in 1740, after which it was sold to Thomas Griffin, Esq; Vice Admiral of the White, whose second son, the Reverend Dr. Griffin of Hadnock near Monmouth, is its present owner.

This celebrated castle was nearly square, covering a space of ground forty eight yards by fifty two, it was defended at each angle by four large round towers, one of which formed an irregular Heptagon. Through a perfect Gothic arch, we are led to a spacious hall of good proportion overgrown with ivy,

adjoin-

adjoining which is an area, presenting the remains of a lofty square building, with circular arched windows in the Saxon style, resembling Gundulph's tower at Rochester castle. By the fragment of a stone staircase, we ascend another embattled tower, through which at a great depth appears the immense fosse, or trench, which is hewn out of a solid rock, and is twenty yards in breadth. Here was once a draw-bridge and two gates with recesses between each, evidently intended as places of safety for its guards, who unseen might annoy the enemy. The various points from which this castle may be viewed to advantage, would afford ample matter for the antiquary, artist, and military architect.

QUITTING this spot, several views of the castle presented themselves, but they were all undignified and uninteresting when compared with those we had before contemplated

plated. The country on the opposite side of the river to and the village of Walford, is peculiarly beautiful. In the church of Walford, one of the aisles is now called Kyrle's chapel, it was erected by that family for their private use, before it became a parochial church; about a mile below the castle, is a small remain of Goodrich priory; a few Gothic windows are yet standing, and part of the chapel which is now converted to a granary; the whole affords an object sufficient to attract the notice of the curious.

This priory was a monastery of the order of black cannons regular of St. Augustine, founded and endowed with the king's licence in the twentieth of Edward the fourth, 1347. Its situation corresponds with the happy choice usually made by the ancient possessors of religious houses, it stands in a fertile valley, watered by one of the finest rivers in the kingdom. The building with the lands contiguous to the castle are occupied by a Mr. Bellamy. From the ascent, approaching the village of Goodrich, a rich and extensive view presents itself across the forest of Dean, from whence Rure-dean church happily breaks upon the eye.

HERE the Wye in a long and serpentine reach, appears in a perspective point of view and affords a pleasing and happy termination to the scenery; its banks are screened on the south, by an extensive coppice wood, and on the

the north, by fertile meadows rifing towards Bifhops-wood, from which a confiderable ... furnace in this vicinity derives its name. ... quarries in ... g noor- ... ew bridge at Briftol was princi- ... erected.

PASSING down the river, the next object that attracts our notice is Courtfield, the feat of the Vaughan family.

THIS fpot is rendered remarkable from Henry the fifth having been nurfed in the neighbourhood. That prince we are told, was when young of a weak and fickly habit, and was placed under the care of a countefs of Salifbury, from which circumftance in all probability, the original name of this place which was Greyfield, was changed to the appellation it now bears. We next approach Lidbroke colliery and very large and extenfive wharf, from whence a confiderable

commerce

commerce in coals is carried on to Rofs, Hereford and other places. This productive mine is the property of Lord Gage. With all the dark and dingy attributes of this place, involved as it is in fmoke, and begirt with coal barges, it yet affords a very pleafing and interefting landfcape. The high road that afcends the woody hill, fcreening the back ground of this wharf, is perpetually enlivened by horfes and carriages in this footy fable commerce, while on the bank of the river beneath, the lading and unlading the veffels, afford additional bufinefs and variety to the fcene. This view is finely contrafted on a fudden bend of the river a little below, where all is tranquil and ferene. The picturefque village of Welch Bicknor prefents itfelf in a rich valley on the right bank of the Wye, happily overfhaded by a thicket of woods, ranged in a grand and circular fweep. Thefe are called

M   Hawk-

Hawkwood and Packwood, and extend about a mile along the bank of the river. The village church and parsonage house, group in a form peculiarly beautiful and interesting.

In the body of the church, fronting the reading desk, is a cumbent whole length female figure, well sculptured in a darkish coloured stone. Traditional report says it represents the countess of Salisbury, whom we have just mentioned as having nursed king Henry the fifth. She holds a child in each arm. This effigy is highly worthy of notice. The drapery is in a loose and free style, and the general contour of the whole bespeaks it the work of an artist of talent. A little below this fane, the Wye is bounded on the opposite shore by a long range of hills, beautifully cloathed with verdure, and diversified by a rich and broken soil of a warm and reddish hue, frequently over clouded with shades of smoak that issue from the various kilns, kept continually burning near this spot. These circumstances trifling and adventitious as they may appear, give relief and effect to the picturesque and beautiful in landscape. Approaching the foot of Cold-well rocks, a scene sublime and majestic presents itself. The grand prominencies are overhung with richly varied tufts of oak, and other shrubberies, occasionally contrasted and relieved by deep and shadowy dells, formed by the various lime kilns on their surface. Some of the most prominent of Cold-well rocks, we are informed have by some gentlemen of the bar, in their passage down this river, been christened after the names of our principal council. The connection is not obvious, or readily traced.

Here we quitted the barge to ascend these majestic rocks, which by an immense and craggy steep, we with difficulty accomplished, and reached the summit called Symond's Gate. This task, arduous as it is should not not deter the traveller from pursuing this course, as by means of it he will avoid a dull and uninteresting passage on the water of full three miles to the new Weir, and by passing over these rocks he will enjoy a sublimity of scenery that will amply repay his toil and labour. As we ascend these superb masses of stone, the rich and extensive scenery that surrounds us, is every moment unfolding itself: the summit is richly overgrown with wild thyme, and variegated flowers, and is crowned with the rich and deep foliage of the noble oak

" Here all the air a solemn stillness holds"

save the distant lowing of cattle, and from
his

his rocky bed, the dirge like evening song of the owl, that floats along the gale.

From hence Goodrich castle, which we imagined we had left far behind, breaks suddenly upon the eye, and appears from the immense winding of the river to be a near object. The new weir, and adjoining waterfall, with the surrounding rich and healthy hills afford from this spot a combination of objects, that deservedly rank among the first views on the river, or perhaps in this country.

The village of Whitechurch in the centre of the vale beneath, with the vast hills beyond it, afford a sublime termination to this reach of the river.

At Whitechurch is a second ferry called Hunson's Rope. This ferry although seven miles

miles distant by water from that of Goodrich, is only one mile by land, a striking instance of the very appropriate and characteristical title of our river, which from its mazy and circuitous course, is justly denominated the Vaga, or Wye.

SECTION VII.

DESCENDING towards the new Weir by a courſe not leſs rugged than that by which we aſcended, the fatigue we had undergone, was amply repaid by the gratification we received in ſome of the moſt beautiful views that can be imagined. Theſe preſented themſelves through the various breaks of the rocks, or openings of the ſurrounding woods with which they are enriched. The ſerpentine winding of the river, and the vaſt prominencies and fantaſtic forms of the rocks in its vicinity, give an air of ſolemn gloom and grandeur to the ſcene. From the approach to the Weir, the annexed view was ſelected, it compriſes all the principal objects that could be admitted within the limits of a ſcale ſo circumſcribed. The innumerable circum-

ſtances

stances that aid this grand and sublime scene, are such as to render it almost impossible for the pencil, to render it justice The iron forges on the opposite side of the river, not less from their appearance than from the important purposes they answer in human life, give an interest to this ef- of nature, while the awful sound of the iron hammers beating the fiery mass, awakens in the mind new sensations giving dignity and grandeur to the subject. This picturesque scene is much heightened by the immense volumes of sparkling smoak that are continually issuing from the forges, these give a pleasing though transitory relief to the sombre, and distant hills that terminate the view. Around these works are scattered great masses of half burned ore, coal, and cinders, and intersperfed on the barren and extensive moor in the vicinity, are many humble cottages of the various workmen employed in the manufactory.

tory. The roaring of the waters from the cascade of the Weir adjoining to this work has a grand effect, its fall is precipitate although at no great height, nor is it perceived from above the stream.

The river here receives a considerable degree of agitation from the huge masses of stone, either swept down by the stream, or hurled from the summit of the neighbouring rocks. Here the Wye increases in width, and its current is so strong, that it is with extraordinary labour and difficulty the barges are towed up. I have seen eight or ten men throwing themselves on the earth on every pull, to give force to their exertions.

In this part of the river is frequently seen a small fishing boat on a singular construction, called a corricle, it is ribbed with laths or split twigs, and is covered with a strong

strong pitched canvas, to prevent its leaking, it is about five feet and a half long and four broad. In the middle is a feat that holds one man, who fits with a paddle in one hand while he fishes with the other. His labour finished, he throws the corricle over his shoulder and retires to his home.

A little below the weir the river scenery is terminated by what is called King Arthur's plain, or Doward hills. To the traveller who is bold enough to attempt the summit of these hills, the views will afford ample variety both in the beautiful and sublime. Camden conjectures, that on these hills there has anciently been a fortification, and what makes it more probable is, that in digging there for iron ore, and lime stone, he says " broad arrow heads have " been found, and not long ago, the great- " est part of the bones of a gigantic per- " son were found here interred, in a place
" that

"that seemed to be arched over." Whatever may have been the ancient deftination of this fpot, its prefent attractions proceed from the very extenfive and richly diverfified profpects that prefent themfelves from every point of view. On a fpot adjoining to the wood on the extremity of this hill, is a cavern that bears the name of King Arthur's Hall; it is faid to extend by a fubteraneous paffage from hence to the new weir, a diftance of about a mile. Many fabulous and romantic tales have been attached to the hiftory of this hall, but the fact appears to be fimply this, that it was a cavern, from whence was dug a rich mine of iron ore, that fupplied the adjoining furnaces.

A DETACHED clufter of rocks called St. Martins', or the three Sifters, fomewhat refembling but much inferior to thofe at Coldwell, fkirt the river in paffing down, near which

which at a short reach called St. Martin's Well, the stream is supposed to have a greater depth of water than in any other part. At the extremity of this reach from a beautiful vale, King Arthur's plain again presents itself, assuming a new and castellated form, and here every stroak of the oar gives variety to the scene, and every object seems to vary its situation. The vast assemblage of rocks we have just contemplated, appear to vanish and melt into a distant hill, rising from a craggy base on the margin of the river.

About two miles before we reach Monmouth, Hadnock house and the beauties of its situation justly demand our attention. It is situated on the edge of the forest of Dean, and stands on the brow of a hill, commanding a fascinating view of the meandering Wye, that gently glides beneath its rocky hills: these are enriched with verdant

dant coppice woods that fcreen this beautiful fpot, the refidence of the Rev. Dr. Griffin, whom we have before mentioned. From hence along the bafe of the hills, a road running parallel with the river that leads on to Monmouth.

SECTION VIII.

QUITTING Hadnock, we are gratified with a diſtant view of the bridge and town of Monmouth. The ſolitary church of Dixton on the oppoſite bank of the river, although deficient in accompaniments is yet a characteriſtic and intereſting feature in the fore ground of the landſcape; and it continues to be ſuch, though ſince this drawing was executed, its interior received in the great flood in 1795 very material injury; the water having forced its way through the windows and doors, and torn up th pulpit, pews and pavement.

MONMOUTH bridge is of ſtone, and conſiſts of ſix irregular arches. The town derives its name from its ſituation at the

conflux

conflux of the Wye and Mynwye, generally, and by the Welſh particularly pronounced Monnow.

A GREAT part of Monmouth is encompaſſed by this river which empties itſelf into the Wye at the lower end of the town; where a very ancient bridge and gateway, formerly a barrier againſt the Welſh, is thrown acroſs this mountain ſtream. It is ſomewhat extraordinary, that neither hiſtory or tradition, although they are both mentioned by Leland in his itinerary, afford any information as to the period in which they were built. Independent however of hiſtorical evidence, they bear ſuch unequivocal marks of antiquity, that the picturefque effect they produce, gives them ample claim to a place in this work. The annexed plate will we flatter ourſelves, convey a faithful repreſentation of this venerable remain, and

in

in some degree illustrate the situation of the town itself; which though low, is seated in a spot at once both pleasing and romantic.

Monmouth had anciently four gates, and the suburb was defended by a wall and deep ditch on each side, except that next the river. As far back as Leland's time, the walls and every other embattled part but the square tower were in a state of ruin. The church is an entire modern structure.

Monmouth has high claim to consideration and respect, from its having given birth to our fifth Henry the conqueror of France, whose active spirit, warlike qualities, and superior skill in horsemanship, particularly at a time when to be accomplished, was indispensible to the character of a gentleman, and the cavalry service began to be in a manner appropriated to men of this rank,

rank, are thus enchantingly, and with all the ease and grace of the gallant and princely horseman he describes, delineated by our matchless bard.

"I saw young Harry with his beaver on,
"His cuisses on his thighs, gallantly arm'd,
"Rise from the ground like feather'd Mercury,
"And vaulted with such ease into his seat
"As if an angel dropp'd down from the clouds,
"To turn and wind a fiery pegasus,
"And witch the world with feats of horsemanship."

HENRY was born in the castle of Monmouth, of which little more remains than a few fragments of walls, and an elevation or mound of earth, just sufficient to ascertain its site; and to demonstrate how evanescent and transitory are all human things; the strong embattled fortress as well as the cradle of princes. Such once were to be found on this spot; and that this awful truth may be more strongly impressed and exemplified,
though

though there yet remains more visible and palpable evidence of one than of the other, let it be remembered, that the record of history will retain the memory of the birth place of Henry, when all traces of the castle shall have passed away, and even its site shall as ineffectually be sought after as at this hour the image of its former splendour.

In this castle Edward the second, after he had been made prisoner by his queen Isabella, in 1326, was for a time confined. Having in the south west direction of the town, with some difficulty obtained a sketch of the ruin of the castle that partakes much of the picturesque, it is here given as an illustration of this venerable spot. The river Monnow beautifully winds beneath its ruined walls, the wooden bridge that is thrown across the stream, and the rich and verdant scenery of its hilly bank, all conspire to produce a landscape highly deserving a
place

place in this work. The remains of the castle, denote it to be of Roman construction, Camden says that from the king's records, a castle was standing here in a flourishing state, as early as the time of William the Conqueror, and that it was rebuilt by John Baron of Monmouth, about the year 1240.

This town has not only the honor of giving birth to a great king, but likewise to a great historian, Galfredius Arthurius, Bishop of St. Asaph, better known by the name of Jeffery of Monmouth. He is supposed to have been educated at this place, which had then a benedictine monastery, or convent of black monks, founded in 1240 by Wihenoe de Monemue, or Monmouth. Monasteries were at that time the principal seminaries for learning in this country, as Oxford and Cambridge had not then risen to any great celebrity, and were at that period much depressed in consequence of the Da-
nish

nish invasion. Jeffery was made arch deacon of Monmouth in 1251, and was soon afterwards created bishop of St. Asaph. He translated the history of Britain from the British language into Latin, a work said to have been discovered by Walter Mapæus while in Armorica, and brought by him into England, where meeting with Jeffery of Monmouth, a man profoundly versed in the history and antiquities of Britain, and an elegant writer for the period in which he lived the task was entrusted to him. Merlin's prophecies he also translated from British verse into Latin prose. This work was of essential service to the Welch chieftain Owen Glendwr, whose high pretensions to soveriegnty were constantly favoured and cherished by these prophecies. The veracity of Jeffery, as an historian, has been doubted by many; Camden says that his relation of Brutus and his successors ought to be intirely disregarded. It may however be observed

served in favour of this writer, from the testimony of Giraldus Cambrensis his contemporary, that at that period the Welch bards and minstrels from early traditional accounts, received and transmitted with a mixture of religious reverence and awe, solemnly repeated the genealogy of their princes and heroes, from Roderic the Great to Æneas, and from Æneas lineally to Adam.

If this should not altogether be thought to add much to their probable authenticity, it will serve to warrant the introduction of the history, to shew at least that he was not the author of the fiction; and, in tracing the origin of nations, tales to the full as fabulous are to be met with in the pages of many of our gravest and approved writers.

To the few early historians of our own we owe much, and amongst these Jeffery deserves every respect, and we are bound to regret

regret that in succeeding times, the best histories of this country will be found to have been the labors of foreigners. A fragment of Monmouth Priory, we have preserved as a tribute to the memory of the historian who was there educated. The Gothic window that appears in view remains very perfect, and appertains to a venerable ancient chamber, which he is reported to have occupied as a study. From the nature of its foundation, the free school at Monmouth particularly deserves our notice. Burton, in his history of Wales, gives this relation of William Jones its founder: he says, " Wm. Jones was born at
" Monmouth, and forced to quit his coun-
" try for not being able to pay ten groats.
" Coming to London he became first a
" porter, and then a factor; and going
" over to Hamburgh, had such a vent for
" Welch cottons, that he gained a very
" considerable estate in a short time. He
" founded

"founded a fair school in Monmouth, allowing fifty pounds yearly to the master, and a hundred pounds salary to a lecturer, besides a stately alms house for twenty poor people, each of them having two rooms and a garden, and half a crown a week; all which he left to the oversight of the company of haberdashers in London, who discharge their trust therein to this day." Another account of the founder is thus given, but with less credibility. That he was a native of Newland, a few miles distant from Monmouth, and having quitted it when young to seek his fortune, he returned at an advanced period of life, in an apparent state of indigence, although very rich, and applied to his native town for relief as a pauper, which being refused, he took his revenge on the people by retiring to Monmouth, and there dispensing that wealth, that was intended to enrich his native place.

We cannot quit the pleasant town of Monmouth without noticing the massive pile of its goal. Built in a lofty and healthy spot, and in the form of an ancient castle; it frowns over the country, and impresses the idea of rigorous confinement and the impossibility of escape. At the time we visited this expensive and spacious work, it contained only one solitary inhabitant, and he a prisoner for only a very trivial offence. As our goals increase in magnitude, it is with pleasure we have frequently had occasion to remark that there is a decrease of inhabitants, nor is it less worthy of observation that the humanity of supplying even those who least deserve it, with decent accommodation, as well as the blessing of light and air, before denied to them, is now most liberally granted.

Perhaps it may not be too much to infer from hence, that the immensity of the bulk

bulk of thefe buildings, in the confpicuous fituation in which they are now placed, may imprefs the multitude with fuch a terror of the confequence of crimes, as in fome degree to prevent a commiffion of them. This building ftands on an eminence, and commands a fine view of the town and furrounding country.

SECTION IX.

QUITTING Monmouth on an excursion to Rhaglan Castle, we ascended a considerable hill about a mile from the town, that afforded one of the most luxuriant landscapes we had witnessed in the course of our route. From this eminence, the rich valley in which Monmouth is situated, and the beauties of the surrounding country, are highly illustrative of Gray's opinion of the charming situation of this place. He rapturously describes this scene as " the delight of his eyes and the very " seat of pleasure." We have attempted to give an idea of this much admired spot in the annexed plate.

The ride to Rhaglan Castle, a distance of about

about six miles, amply gratified us for this deviation from our main pursuit.

This magnificent remain of ancient splendor stands on an elevated situation commonly called Twyn-y-ciros, which signifies in Welch the cherry hill; and, as we approach it from the village, appears to wear that solemn and majestic air highly characteristic of the spirit of the times in which it flourished. The external view here selected, we flatter ourselves will not only convey the best idea of its extent and magnificence, but is a point from which we do not remember to have ever seen it represented. This noble building, which may rather be terminated a castellated house than a castle, is in many parts, still in good preservation. It was erected in the reign of Henry VII. and does not therefore boast of great antiquity; many additions were made to it about the time of Elizabeth, these

consti-

constitute, the most elegant parts of this superb pile, and are to be found in the windows of the grand hall, or banqueting room; the ornaments of the frieze and cornice are light and elegant, and in the best taste of that time. To the left of this hall, was a large court one hundred feet long, and sixty feet broad, well arched and ornamented, with curious stone work both on the walls and windows. In the midst of the court was a pleasant marble fountain called the White Horse: the following remark of Dr. Griffin, relative to the white horse may not prove uninteresting. " I re-
" member," says he, " some years ago,
" they used to shew here part of the body
" of a black horse, which stood in the
" middle of some water that supplied the
" castle, and was a fountain. I was told
" the parliamentarians poisoned the water
" during the siege, and that the stone horse
" absorbed the poison; it was very hard,
" but

" but on being struck, or rubbed with any
" hard subſtance, emitted a very offenſive
" ſmell. Perhaps I had the legend very
" imperfectly, and it ſhould have been ad-
" ded, the poiſon turned the white horſe
" into a black one." The caſtle is ſur-
rounded by a wide foſſé thirty feet broad, wherein was originally placed an artificial water work, which ſpouted up water to the height of the caſtle, and contains within it two acres, one of which appears to have been encompaſſed with domeſtic offices, ſuch as kitchen, brewhouſe, &c. and in which there is an oven, and fire range of ſuch extraordinary dimenſions, as to ſatisfy us, that there were times in which they were not wholly occupied in feats of arms.

In this building every precaution has been uſed to guard and ſecure the approaches to it ; and the utmoſt magnificence is to be obſerved in every part of the interior, even

in

in the domestic offices. The staircase and ascent to the grand apartments are peculiarly noble; and beneath the areas which are vaulted, are various subterraneous apartments, and extensive cellars of the most excellent workmanship. The citadel, which is octagonal, is surrounded by a moat, and stands at a small distance from the castle: its principal parts are in a perfect state of preservation. This noble castle is in the possession of the Duke of Beaufort, whose ancestor, the Marquis of Worcester in the time of Charles the first, added and fortified many extensive out works, by which he was enabled to hold it for the king's use till his imprisonment at Holmby. It once contained a garrison of eight hundred men, and was the last castle that surrendered to the parliament forces, then under the command of Sir Thomas Fairfax. This event happened on the nineteenth of August 1646, and is reported to have been effected by a female

male in the garrison, and by the the use of a very ordinary female engine, the mere waving a handkerchief, as a signal for the introduction of Cromwell's party. If this were so, politics were probably by no means the primary incentives of this lady's zeal, and there were doubtless secret articles in this treaty, unknown to the besieging general. The window at which she appeared is still shewn.

THE more probable account is, that from the very long siege it sustained, the upper part was undermined, and the timbers being burnt a great part of it fell down. Soon after its surrender, the castle was demolished and left, in nearly the same state in which it now remains. The loss to the family is supposed to be upwards of a hundred thousand pounds, besides the forfeiture of an estate of twenty thousand a year. Three considerable parks of remarkable fertility

tility, and richly stocked with deer, once appertained to this castle.

RETURNING to Monmouth we resumed our passage down the Wye, on a morning, one of the most beautiful ever beheld. The retrospective view of Monmouth on passing down, the spire of the church, the town, bridge, and surrounding scene, though inferior to that above, yet in some respects exhibited a very picturesque landscape. The hills opposite to Monmouth, are called the Kemmin Rocks, on the summit of which Mr. Philip Hardwick, an architect, has erected a stone building for the reception of his friends, called Philip's Court. This spot commands a view most extensive and diversified, and will well repay the labour of climbing up what John Bunyan would justly call *Hill Difficulty*. To those who visit this spot it may be worth the trouble of going about a mile further to view, amongst many others, an immense large rock called the Buck Stone; a name probably derived from the deer having sheltered themselves under it when the adjacent country was in the form of a park. Its situation is on the extreme edge of the hill; and, though of an immense size, it stands on an angular point, and is so nicely balanced, as to be with a very small degree of force, set in motion and shaken. Approaching the junction of the Monnow with the Wye, the side scenes of the river, increase in richness both of woody, and verdant scenery, and with such agreable breaks in the distance as to produce an enchanting effect.

A LITTLE below this point, a small river called the Trothe, or Trothey, unites itself with our Wye, on whose banks they jointly pass, near a a respectable mansion called

called Troy-house, in the possession of the Duke of Beaufort, to whom it descended from Sir Charles Somerset.

Sir Charles was the third son of Edward Earl of Worcester, and married the daughter and heiress of Sir William Powell of Troy, by whom he acquired a considerable estate, and added much influence to the house of Worcester. The present edifice notwithstanding it was designed by Inigo Jones, has little that can recommend it to notice. It is used merely as a lodge, and is occasionally only occupied by the family. A few portraits decorate its walls, but they are not of consequence sufficient to take the traveller far out of his way. The cradle wherein Harry of Monmouth is reported to have been rocked is here exhibited as a great curiosity, but the freshness of its velvet, its nails and appendages, bespeak it rather to have been the receptable of one of the Beaufort family in the time of Charles the second.

To thofe however who are fond of cradles (and in their fecond childhood, amongft our old lady antiquaries, fome fuch there may be) the annexed fketch of one, the appearance of which befpeaks it as not unlikely to have been of that time, and which is in the poffeffion of the Reverend Mr. Ball of Newlands, a few miles from Monmouth, may not prove an unacceptable regale.

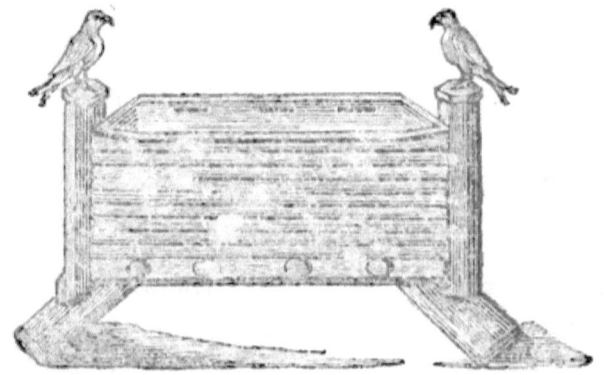

It is made of oak without any covering, and is suspended by two iron rings, by which it receives motion on the least touch or action of the child; it is three feet long, one foot four deep, and one foot six wide; it is ornamented at the top of the supporters, which are octagonal, with two birds, resembling eagles, but their beaks are broken off. The following anecdote relative to Troy house, extracted from the "Apo-" thegms of the Earl of Worcester," it is presumed will be thought not unworthy a place in this work.

" Sir Thomas Somerset, brother to the
" Marquis of Worcester, had a house which
" was called Troy, five miles from Rhaglan
" castle. This Sir Thomas being a com-
" plete gentleman, delighted much in fine
" gardens and orchards, where by the bene-
" fit of art, the earth was made so grateful
" to him at the same time, that the king
" (Charles

"(Charles the firſt) happened to be at his
"brother's houſe, that it yielded him where-
"withal to ſend his brother a preſent; and
"ſuch an one as (the times and the ſeaſons
"conſidered) was able to make the king
"believe, that the ſovereign of the planets
"had now changed the poles, and that
"Wales (the refuſe and the outcaſt of the
"fair garden of England) had fairer and
"riper fruit than England's bowels had
"on all her beds. This preſent, given to
"the marquis, he would not ſuffer to be
"preſented to the king by any hand but
"his own. In comes the marquis then, at
"the end of the ſupper, led by the arm,
"with a ſlow pace, expreſſing much Spaniſh
"gravity, with a ſilver diſh in each hand,
"filled with rarities; and a little baſket on
"his arm as a reſerve, when making his
"obeiſance he thus ſpeaks: May it pleaſe
"your Majeſty, if the four elements could
"have been robbed to have entertained your
"Majeſty,

" Majesty, I think I had but done my duty,
" but I must do as I may. If I had sent
" to Bristol for some good things to enter-
" tain your Majesty, that would have been
" no wonder at all. If I had procured
" from London, some goodness that might
" have been acceptable to your Majesty, that
" would have been no wonder. But here I
" present you, Sir, (placing his dishes upon
" the table) with that which came not from
" Lincoln that was, nor London that is,
" nor York that is to be, but from Troy."
Whereupon the king smiled and answered
the marquis; " Truly my Lord, I have heard
" that corn grows where Troy town stood ;
" but I never thought there had grown any
" apricots before." Whereupon the marquis replied, " Any thing to please your
" Majesty." When my lord marquis departed the presence, one told him that he
would make a very good courtier; remember well, replied the marquis, that I said

one

one thing which may give some hopes of me: *Any thing* to please your majesty.

AMIDST a rich though hilly scenery, beautiful in its forms and happily diversified by a multitude of small farms, that exhibit evident marks of improving cultivation in this, yet very improvable, though fertile country, we reach Redbrook. Here a considerable manufactory of iron and tin gives a new and pleasing variety to the scenery and bustle on our river. Some of the iron ore used here comes from Coldford, and other places in the neighbourhood of the forest of Dean, but the greater part is brought from Lancashire.

ABOUT a mile and a half below Redbrook, the Wye receives a further supply from a small stream called Whitebrook; about the distance of a mile from whence stands St. Briaval's Castle. It is situated on an eminence, and though fo near the river, is from the water too indistinct an object for the pencil. This is to be regretted, as the woody declivities on each side of it are beautiful in their forms, and display a scene uncommonly rich and elegant; but on quitting the boat we found a nearer view of the castle, well worthy a place in this work, and a proper ornament of its subject. The annexed sketch exhibits a north east view of the castle, and the remains of the moat that in part surrounded it.

The distant Monmouthshire hills form a good termination to the scene, while the adjoining church and general face of the landscape presents a view, in its style and and character, materially varying from any we have yet met with. From the remains of this castle it appears to have been a place of great strength, and of considerable extent; it was built by Miles, Earl of Hereford,

ford, in the reign of King Henry I. whose third son named Mahel, Camden informs us, was here overtaken by " God's judg-
" ments for his rapacious ways, inhuman
" cruelties, and boundless avarice. For
" being courteously entertained here by
" Walter de Clifford, the caſtle taking fire,
" he loſt his life by the fall of a ſtone on
" his head, from the higheſt tower." The cuſtody of St. Briaval's, with the Foreſt of Dean, was granted to John de Monemouth, in the eighteenth year of King John. The Earl of Berkeley is the preſent conſtable, and the Duke of Beaufort, under whoſe direction the caſtle is kept in a good ſtate of repair, is lord of the manor. The tower in the weſt front is now uſed as a priſon. From hence, the views of the ſurrounding country are extenſive and beautiful; and here the meandering of the Wye paints the landſcape, as in its general courſe, and ſpreads richneſs and fertility in the vallies

through

through which it flows. Returning to our boat we paſſed Big's Weir, near which, on the bank of the Wye, is the ſeat of General Rooke, whoſe father captured Gibraltar.

It is ſituated in the midſt of a rich paſturage, and commands a full view of the river, and that intereſting variety of moving objects, which its buſy commerce here preſents. Amidſt a range of beautiful ſcenery, we paſs the pleaſant village of Llandogar about a mile below. Here the river forms a ſmooth and glaſſy bay, through which the white ſailed veſſel is ſeen conſtantly gliding, or lying moored on the ſhore to take in her freight. The undulating hills, called the Hudnells, form a beautiful back ground to this charming ſcene, of which the annexed view will give a faint idea.

A little below is Cadithil Weir, from whence we dropped pleaſantly down the stream

stream to another village called Brook's Weir, which is confidered a half way diftance from Monmouth to Chepftow. At this place the goods fent from Monmouth are fhipped and conveyed in larger veffels to Briftol. The river, in an eafy meandering courfe, foon brought us within view of the moft picturefque object on its banks, the fplendid and very elegant ruin of Tintern Abbey,

> "Thefe are fair fcenes where if art whilom trod,
> "Led by the worft of guides fell tyranny,
> "And with lefs fuperftition, we now trace
> "Her footfteps with delight; and pleas'd revere
> "What once we fhould have hated."

APPROACHING this fublime and fequeftered fpot, the enthufiaftic lover of fimplicity in art and nature, the admirer of the picturefque and beautiful, the antiquary and the moralift will feel the effect, as it were, of enchantment, and become loft almoft in a pleafing melancholy. The fleepy hills,

hills, the hanging woods, the rolling stream, the nodding ruin, the surviving monuments of fallen grandeur and beauty in decay; the constructed space, the stillness and retirment, all conspire to imprefs the mind with awe, and for a moment withdraw from its vain purfuit of wealth and power, and abftract it from the world. On this remain, a very able writer has remarked, that " were the building ever fo beautiful, in- " compaffed as it is with fhabby houfes, it " could make no appearance from the ri- " ver." In this we effentially differ, and prefent the annexed view in fupport of our opinion. Here every cottage appears as it really exifts on the fpot; and the petty, or if you pleafe paltry accompaniments to which he alludes, appear to us fo far from diminifhing the grandeur of the general effect, that they ferve rather on the contrary as a fcale, and give magnitude to the principal object.

THE

The ruined windows, pillars, and mouldings are all of them very elegant specimens of the moſt perfect ſtyle of Gothic architecture. That wreck and deſolation to which the revolution of opinion, the waſteful rapacity and tyranny of Henry, had ſubjected this lovely ſpot, would have preſented only marks of violence, and under the pretence of religion, the ravaging arm of an unprincipled barbarian. It is to the gentler tyranny, the ſilent and progreſſive ravages, of time, that we owe many of thoſe delicate touches and features of beauty that embelliſh this elegant and intereſting ruin. Theſe have contributed to ſoften down the ſharper edges of the chiſſel, and, by blending its variegated tufts of moſs, and ſpreading and overhanging with its looſe drapery, and many tinted greens, the highly wrought ornaments and ſculpture of the place, have given to the whole a richneſs and mellowneſs, far beyond the reach of art.

THE

The small gothic Gate at the entrance from the water, was evidently an adjunct of the abbey, and the remaining small buildings adjoining, formed part of its out-offices. The abbey was founded A. D. 1131. by Walter de Clare, for monks of the Ciftercian order; and dedicated to Saint Mary. About the time of the revolution, here were thirteen religious houfes, whofe eftates were eftimated according to Dugdale at one hundred and ninety-two pounds, one fhilling and four pence per annum. The fite was granted in the twenty-eighth of Henry the VIII. to Henry Earl of Worcefter, from whom it has defcended to the prefent Duke of Beaufort.

On entering this fublime ruin the mind is ftruck with a reverential and religious awe : a fenfation which can be no more expreffed by words, than it can in this full extent be excited by all the graces of Grecian
propor-

proportions, and all the decencies of orthodox worship. The noble clustered columns form a beautiful scene in perspective; and, while some of the rich Gothic ornaments and pointed arches above, present themselves as if magically suspended, and raise an idea of grandeur, accompanied, if not with alarm with some degree of surprise, the various ruinated fragments of capitals and pillars below, which lie scattered indiscriminately and in part overgrown and buried in beds of wild flowers and verdant tendrils, create an interesting disorder, and suggest ideas, though perhaps of a melancholy tinge, yet so far from a distressing nature as to lull the mind to a repose, congenial to the general turn of the surrounding scenery.

The smooth and trim manner in which the ground is here kept, is not, according to our conception, very much in unison with the assemblage of objects around, where

broken-

brokenneſs and irregularity are the principal and leading features of the place, the tameneſs and uniformity produced by it, are incongruous and out of character.

The weſtern window, although in point of proportion rather too wide for its height, is yet a curious ſpecimen of the ancient Gothic, and no contemptible ſtudy for one who is ſmitten with a true paſſion for the antique. The roof of the building is entirely fallen in, and with it ſome of the pillars are loſt, but their baſes ſtill remain above the ſurface of the ground, ſo as to enable the antiquary, if he has the leaſt of the architect about him, very eaſily to give a ground plot of the whole.

In the middle of the nave, the lofty arches which once ſupported the ſteeple, riſe high above the reſt ; but though they retain their forms, they are reduced to a mere ridge of stone.

The neighbouring iron works belonging to Mr. Tanner of Monmouth, will afford a different scene, and should be visited by every traveller. Here the quiet and repose of the cottage is happily contrasted by the activity and bustle of the forge.

In passing along the river side to the iron works, many beautiful passages in landscape present themselves; they are composed of woody and diversified hills, similar to those adjoining to the abbey, but heightened by the busy scenes of the labourer and artificer, constantly employed in the adjacent manufactory. The iron works are principally supplied from Furness in Lancashire with ore, which is disolved by the blasts of immense bellows that are worked by means

of

of cylinder pumps. The beſt qualities of the ore are ſeparated from the droſs by a water wheel and hammers, by which operation conſiderable quantities of pure metal are collected, and the powder is ſold to the glaſs houſes. Various forges are here contrived for the purpoſe of forming the mutilated ore into proper ſizes, from the largeſt bar of iron, to the ſmalleſt wire.

SECTION X.

BENDING our courfe down the Wye we pafs a promontory, from whence the eaftern extremity of the abbey prefents itfelf; but here all is flat and uninterefting, compared with the fcene we have juft quitted. In this point of view the tottering and folitary pillar, remaining in the centre of the great eaft window, appears to be fcarce able to fupport itfelf; thus circumftanced it is fortunate for the antiquary that very little of the fabric depends upon it, or a great part of that venerable ftructure would, ere long, inevitably come to the ground with it.

WE were foon deprived of any further view of this elegant remain by a ftrong wind and tide, which quickly hurried us
down

down the stream; but scenes like these, on which the mind has long dwelt in pleasing meditation are not easily ...d by a mere change of p.... ..ey on the contrary are rather ci..ished by the preceding scenery, by the gloom of the rock, the repose of the meadow, and the stillness of the gliding stream; nor do they disappear till we mix in the busy hum of men, till we plunge into the more tumultuous scene of human life and human passions.

Having passed much beautiful scenery nearly of the style and character of that which we witnessed about Tintern, here we again discover the eastern bank of the Wye screened with rocky substances, not unlike those at Coldwell. These substances are called the Thorn, and Black Cliffs. The water at this place is much discoloured, and acquires a thick and clayey hue, evidently produced by the influx of the tide, which is here

here very visible, and which from the Severn sea, and the low marshy land on its shores is so impregnated with mud, and imports it in such quantities as to foul the pearly tresses of the Wye, even to a degree of deformity.

>   ——" The torrent flood,
> " Thy molten chrystal fills with mud,
> " Tho' thy lofty head be crown'd
> " With many a tower and terras round."

We now approach the rocks that terminate the grounds of Persfield; these are tremendous projections hanging over the river, and in their form resemble so many bastions of a castle. They are twelve in number, and bear the name of the Twelve Apostles; a thirteenth in the same range is terminated by a slender stone about five feet in height, which is called St. Peter's Thumb. In this spot we are struck with a wonderful reverberation of sound, such as must afford a curious speculation to the

philoso-

philosophical inquirer into the nature and properties of air, and that conformation of earth and rock and woody accompaniment, which are necessary to produce with such continued repercussion, an echo so clear and distinct. A little below these rocks a person, some years ago, fell unhurt from an immense height into the woods on the margin of the river. This almost miraculous interposition on his behalf, wrought very little effect upon his life and manners, for so hardened and incapable was he of being acted upon, either by the recollection of mercies or the dread of punishment, that, having not long after attended the execution of a friend for a robbery, he conceived in his mind the plan of a similar crime, perpetrated it, and suffered the same fate. So that his rescue from a watery grave seems to have served little purpose beyond that of verifying the adage, that he, who is destined to the halter, may brave the precipice and

the

the flood. A little lower down the river we pafs the rocks, from the fudden and precipitate fall they prefent, called the Lover's Leap. Had he not happily been caught by the fhrubbery planted below, Mr. Morris the former poffeffor, had here fallen a facrifice to his paffion for thofe fimple charms of nature, which he explored and dreffed with a correfpondent tafte. He added to their variety without leffening their intereft. Since that time a profeffed improver has been let in, and the confequence, not the *natural* confequence, has been that with his roller and fhears, infipid uniformity has identified the ever changeful fcene; and the flime of this fnail has fcarce lefs deformed its dells, its craggy hills, and its groves, than has the mud of the Severn that polluted its waters. To prevent any fuch accident in future this gentleman foon after fixed a rail on the edge of the precipice. By a fteep and unpleafant path, the traveller, from thefe rocks, has

T   fome-sometimes ascended to the grounds of Persfield. A circular bend of the river now displayed to our view the noble ruin of Chepstow castle. The situation of this venerable building is striking. It is built on the summit of an immense perpendicular rock, into which it appears rivetted, or rather to be growing out of it; as from the top of the battlements, down to the base of the cliff on the margin of the river, it is one continued range of precipice.

This majestic remain, is from the present point of view peculiarly interesting, and in its effect highly picturesque. The ancient Gothic entrance partly in ruin, the irregular breaks and prominencies in the general form of the building, which is a mixture of the Norman and Saxon style, are in many parts overgrown with large clumps of ivy and variegated shrubs, sometimes beautifully clustered among the fragments of the castle.

castle, and again falling down and enriching the white and awful cliff below.

The adjoining bridge from its height, singular construction, and relative situation to the castle has a romantic air, and is well calculated to give general effect to the landscape.

On the opposite shore, the different forms of the cliffs and rich verdure with which they are cloathed, and the masts of the vessels from behind the bridge breaking on the eye, complete the scene, and render it altogether a happy group of objects for the pencil. This bridge is built with timber, and the boards which compose the floor, are so laid as to yield to the water and play some inches. It is seventy feet above the surface of the river, and is so constructed in consequence of the impetuosity of the tide, which, just as it rushes in from the Severn sea, being here suddenly confined within a narrow channel, is frequently known to have risen forty feet. As it divides the counties of Gloucester and Monmouth, it is kept in repair at their joint-expence.

According to some accounts, Chepstow castle appears formerly to have occupied a considerable space of ground, not less it is presumed than five acres. About six hundred years since, it was rebuilt by Gilbert Earl of Pembroke, surnamed Strongbow. This Gilbert was second son of Gilbert de Clare, from him it came after various grants to Charles Somerset, a son of the third Duke of Beaufort, afterwards Earl of Worcester, and from him it descended to the present duke.

The premises have been for many years under a lease for lives, the last of which

which is at prefent in 1794, an aged woman who fhews the caftle in which fhe was born. Amongft the feveral buildings ftill remaining, the chapel demands attention, it is fpacious and has been much ornamented. Twelve large niches with finicircular arches over them, are formed in the walls. They have feats which are chair high above the floor. The ufes to which they were appropriated is not clearly afcertained. The grand entrance on the eaft fide, is a noble and venerable remain of the Norman ftile of building, it ftands between two lofty towers, and is in a good ftate of prefervation. Much of the Roman wall, in the north weft angle of the chapel, appears in the courfes of bricks between the ftone facings.

In the civil diffentions of the laft century, this caftle was confidered of great importance

portance to both parties, and a garrison was continued here after the restoration. A spacious apartment is still shewn in which Henry Martin, one of the king's judges, was confined a close prisoner for twenty seven years.

The life of this remarkable man was spared, he having surrendered himself conformable to the proclamation issued, when that event took place. His estates in Berkshire, which were considerable, were sequestered, and here he resided till 1680, when according to Anthony Wood, he died suddenly while at dinner, at the age of 78. He was buried in Chepstow church, and on his tomb stone were engraved the following lines. As they are now obliterated and are said to have been written by himself, they may be thought worth preserving. The Epitaph is an Acrostic.

HERE, SEPTEMBER THE NINTH,

WAS BURIED

A TRUE ENGLISHMAN,

Who in Berkſhire, was well known
To love his country's freedom 'bove his own;
But being immured full twenty year,
Had time to write as doth appear.

HIS EPITAPH.

H ere or elſewhere, (all's one to you, to me
E arth, air, or water, gripes my ghoſtly duſt,
N one knows how ſoon to be by fire ſet free:
R eader if you an oft try'd rule will truſt,
Y ou'll gladly do and ſuffer what you muſt.

M y time was ſpent in ſerving you, and you
A nd death's my pay, it ſeems, and welcome too,
R evenge deſtroying but itſelf, while I,
T o birds of prey leave my old cage and fly.
E xamples preach to the eye: care then, mine ſays,
N ot how you end, but how you ſpend your days.

Some years after its interment, by order of the then clergyman, the body was removed to an obſcure ſituation, that the church

church might not be disgraced by containing the ashes of a regicide. Chepstow church, formed a part of the old priory belonging to the Benedictine monks founded in the reign of King Stephen. Leland says this was a cell to Bermondsey abbey, but it does not appear to be so in the First Fruits Office; as no rent, or pension by way of acknowledgement, is there recorded to that abbey.

The style of building of this church is pure Norman, the arches of the nave are circular, which are supported by square massive pillars in a very perfect state. The entrance to the west front is in a very fine style, of the same architecture, the proportions are just, and the pillars and mouldings are richly decorated in the taste of that period. As we have quoted one monumental inscription, from this ancient receptacle of the dead, we flatter ourselves that we may without making an obituary of this work, be be permitted to contract the two following. The first was on a sea captain, who died in 1774.

> The blusterous blasts, and Neptune's waves,
>   Have tost me too, and fro;
> In spite of all, by God's decree
>   I harbour here below.
> Here I am anchor'd with many of our fleet,
> But we shall sail again, our Admiral Christ to meet.

The following is on John Davis, a jockey of this town, who seems determined in his technical phrases to outdo, not only the captain, but to distance all that may hereafter be said on the subject.

> 'Tis vain to trust to human strength, or art,
> When God doth strive, ye will small aid impart
> As my mishap, 'tho skill'd in riding, shows
> That the Almighty, horse and rider throws.
> Be then prepar'd, my friends, since accidents
> May in an instant hurry you from hence.

From Chepstow by a very pleasant ride we visited the charming grounds of Persfield

field a spot where nature has been uncommonly profuse, not only in the difposition of the beautiful flopes and waving lawns that enrich and compofe the grounds themfelves, but in the extenfive and diverfified fcenery that ftrikes the eye, from every point of view. I have here felected from amidft a profufion of magnificent and fafcinating objects, rarely to be met with in this or any other country, a very extenfive fketch that includes Chepftow caftle, and the town beneath, together with the rocky cliffs defigned as it were by nature to bound the courfe of the Wye, whofe beautiful meandering extends for a diftance of three miles, and then lofes itfelf in the greater waters of the Severn. Here

——————— " Pleas'd *Vaga* pour'd
" His fea green ftreams, deep murmuring beneath
" The hanging bowers and glittering rocks; while wide
" The rougher Severn ftretch'd his arm, beftrew'd
" With fhining fails, to the capacious ocean."

This enchanting scene is bounded by the Gloucestershire and Somersetshire hills, and affords a subject for landscape, more sublime and picturesque than the most fertile imagination can conceive. An attempt to describe every beautiful object that presents itself within the circuit of these grounds, would in the recital be tedious and uninteresting, I shall therefore only observe, that the scenery on this spot is perpetually diversified, and nature every where rises beyond the reach of art. The enclosed view, though I may in my attempt have merited the praise of fidelity, will I fear convey but a faint and unimpressive idea of that scenery which is adapted only to the talent and pencil of a Claude Lorraine.

In contemplating this magnificent and stupendous assemblage of nature and art, we are led as it were instinctively to deplore the melancholy reverse of fortune, that sad-

deared the laft days of the original defigner and owner of this charming fpot ; of him whofe elegant mind and munificent hand could, out of the rude uncultivated mafs, project and raife to the higheft ftate of perfection a monument of tafte, that muft remain an ornament to his country.

We could not take our leave of Chepftow, without giving a retrofpective view of the caftle, and its tremendous rocky bafe and diftant fcenery over which we had juft paffed. The romantic bridge and bufy fcene on the water, all combined to aid the landfcape, and to give a further illuftration of this fafcinating place. Chepftow, the grand and central port of the commerce of our river, is here finely difplayed by the throng that lined the wharf, and the grove of trading veffels through which we paffed. The lofty and high impending fcreen of rocks, on either fide the river, rendered our paffage

down

down the ftream delightful. Amongft thefe the red rocks and Hardwick cliff are peculiarly attractive, in the latter many large appertures have been dug that are paffable, and extend forty, or fifty yards from the entrance, and in the vicinity is a remarkable fine well of water, that gives the name of Thornwell to a beautiful range of woods, adjoining the termination of Hardwick cliff.

The annexed view of what are called the Red Rocks, will give a general idea of the face of the river, in our paffage down to the mouth of the Wye, where we found the tide uncommonly rapid, and where if the wind is brifk, the waters are troublefomely rough.

It is here matter of much regret, that we cannot with fidelity introduce the diftant Severn, which would have rendered the view more complete. At Ewen's rocks, about

about a mile below, that noble river breaks extensively on the eye, and presents a beautiful scene, but it is altogether an inferior one to that before us.

At the conflux of the Wye, or in the vicinity of Beachley, (the old passage house) the Severn is seen to greater advantage. The distant hills of Gloucestershire and Somersetshire, beautifully intersecting each other in varied tints, while intervening objects of castles, villages, and mansions of the wealthy and great on the opposite shore, richly diversify and compleat the whole. The distance, composed of Walton hills about ten miles below, breaks beautifully on the eye, and forms a happy termination across King's-road and the Bristol channel.

From hence the groups of vessels that are constantly moored near the mouth of the Bristol Avon, although at a distance of near three

three miles, are perfectly diftinguifhable. The immenfe quantity of fhipping perpetually paffing and repaffing before the eye, convey a magnificent idea, both of that celebrated mart of our country, the city of Briftol, and of the extenfive commerce of the Severn, a river, memorable and facred almoft as the wizard Dee in ancient fong; a torrent before the grandeur of whofe flood, our more beautiful Wye feels diminifhed and fubmits her humbler and tributary ftream, a torrent whofe guardian fpirit we fhall at another, and we truft no very diftant day hope to invoke, and with

" Shepherds in the feftival of peace
" Carol her goodnefs loud in ruftic lays,
" And throw fweet garland wreaths into her ftream
" Of panfies, pinks, and gaudy daffodils.

FINIS.

www.ingramcontent.com/pod-product-compliance
Lightning Source LLC
Chambersburg PA
CBHW020244170426
43202CB00008B/218